THEMATIC UNIT
Butterflies

Written By Mary Ellen Sterling

Teacher Created Materials, Inc.
6421 Industry Way
Westminster, CA 92683
www.teachercreated.com
©1999 Teacher Created Materials, Inc.
Reprinted, 2002
Made in U.S.A.
ISBN-1-57690-372-9

Illustrated by
Barb Lorseydi

Edited by
Janet A. Hale, M.S. Ed.

Cover Art by
Chris Macabitas

Table of Contents

Introduction

Butterflies contains a fun-filled, whole-language thematic unit. This 80-page, literature based, thematic unit was designed to immerse children in writing, poetry, language arts, science, math, social studies, music, art, and life skills. The literature and activities used in this thematic unit have been selected to help children gain a better understanding of others and take into consideration other's points of view. A variety of teaching strategies such as cooperative learning, hands-on experiences and child-centered assessment are integrated throughout this thematic unit.

This thematic unit includes the following:

- ❏ **literature selections**—summaries of two children's books with related lessons (complete with reproducible pages) that cross the curriculum

- ❏ **poetry**—suggested selections and lessons enabling children to write and publish their own works

- ❏ **planning guides**—suggestions for sequencing lessons each day of the unit

- ❏ **bulletin board ideas**—suggestions and plans for student-created and/or interactive bulletin boards

- ❏ **curriculum connections**—in language arts, math, science, art, music, and life skills such as cooking

- ❏ **a culminating activity**—which requires students to synthesize their learning to produce a product or engage in an activity that can be shared with others

- ❏ **a bibliography**—suggesting additional literature and nonfiction books on the theme

---

To keep this valuable resource intact so that it can be used year after year, you may wish to punch holes in the pages and store them in a three-ring binder.

Introduction (cont.)

Why a Balanced Approach?

The strength of a whole language approach is that it involves children in using all modes of communication: reading, writing, listening, illustrating, and doing. Communication skills are interconnected and integrated into lessons that emphasize the whole of language. Balancing this approach is our knowledge that every whole - including individual words - is composed of parts, and directed study of those parts can help a child to master the whole. Experience and research tell us that regular attention to phonics, other word-attack skills, spelling, and so forth, develop reading mastery, thereby fulfilling the unity of the whole-language experience. The child is thus led to read, write, spell, speak, and listen confidently in response to a literature experience introduced by the teacher. In these ways, language skills grow rapidly, stimulated by direct practice, involvement, and interest in the topic at hand.

Why Thematic Planning?

One very useful tool for implementing a balanced language program is thematic planning. By choosing a theme with correlating literature selections for a unit of study, a teacher can plan activities throughout the day that lead to a cohesive, in-depth study of the topic. Children will be practicing and applying their skills in meaningful contexts. Consequently, they tend to learn and retain more. Both teachers and children will be freed from a day that is broken into unrelated segments of isolated drill and practice.

Why Cooperative Learning?

Besides academic skills and content, children need to learn social skills. No longer can this area of development be taken for granted. Children must learn to work cooperatively in groups in order to function well in modern society. Group activities should be a regular part of school life, and teachers should consciously include social objectives as well as academic objectives in their planning. For example, a group working together to write a report may need to select a leader. The teacher should make clear to the children and monitor the qualities of good leader-follower group interactions, just as he/she would state and monitor the academic goals of the project.

Why Big Books?

An excellent, cooperative, whole-language activity is the production of Big Books. Groups of children, or the whole class, can apply their language skills, content knowledge, and creativity to produce a Big Book that can become a part of the classroom library to be read and reread. These books make excellent culminating projects for sharing beyond the classroom with parents, librarians, other classes, and so forth. Big Books can be produced in many ways, and this thematic unit book includes directions for at least one method you may choose.

The Very Hungry Caterpillar

by Eric Carle

Summary

This simple yet elegantly-illustrated picture book tells the story of the life cycle of a butterfly. It begins with an egg lying on a leaf. Out of this egg comes a caterpillar, a very hungry caterpillar. It eats more and more food every day and pretty soon it is no longer such a little caterpillar. After building a small house around itself, the caterpillar stays inside for more than two weeks. When it is ready, a beautiful butterfly emerges from the chrysalis and makes its grand entrance into the world.

The outline below is a suggested plan for using the various activities that are presented in this unit. You should adapt these ideas to fit your own classroom situation.

Sample Plan

Lesson 1

- Discuss the relationship between caterpillars and butterflies.
- Review the days of the week.
- Read *The Very Hungry Caterpillar* to the class.
- Let the children make predictions as you read.

Lesson 2

- Retell the story with props (pages 11 to 14).
- Determine what is real and what is make believe (page 15).
- Reinforce counting concepts with the activity found on page 17.
- Make a caterpillar (projects, page 38 and page 67).

Lesson 3

- Review the story with props (pages 11 to 14).
- Complete unfinished sentences utilizing "Writing in the Round" found on page 21.
- Write math story problems and make a class book (page 16).
- Make a butterfly life cycle strip (page 22).

Lesson 4

- Write an innovation of *The Very Hungry Caterpillar* (page 21).
- Put on a butterfly/chrysalis puppet performance (page 11).
- Practice making number sets (game, pages 19 and 20).
- Make tissue paper collages (page 23).

Lesson 5

- For a culminating activity, make a Giant Caterpillar Book (page 24).

Overview of Activities

1. Prepare and assemble some or all of the Setting the Stage resources:

    Bulletin Board: A bulletin board display will help set the mood in your classroom. See pages 74 and 75 for some exciting ideas.

    Butterfly Home: Create your own butterfly home (see page 10 for suggestions) and display in a special classroom center. If caterpillars cannot be located, some sources for obtaining them can be found on page 77.

    Story Props: Make a set of story props from the patterns on pages 12, 13 and 14. Two different methods for constructing the props are explained on page 11, along with several suggested activities.

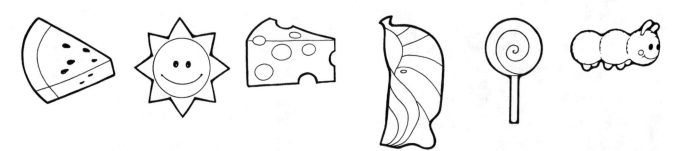

    Literature: Gather all fiction and nonfiction books that you will need. Display them on a special table or in a decorated box. See the Bibliography, pages 79 and 80, for some suggested choices.

    Multimedia: Preview all films and software programs (see page 78), as well as music suggestions (page 65), so you will know which selections will work best with your class.

2. Ask the children to explain what a butterfly is and what a caterpillar is. Talk about how the two are related.

3. Teach or review the days of the week. Discuss some typical activities that might take place on each day. For example, Sunday may be the day their family attends church services; Monday begins the school week, etc.

4. Introduce *The Very Hungry Caterpillar* by showing children the cover of the book. Explain that this book is about how a caterpillar changes.

5. Read the first three pages of *The Very Hungry Caterpillar* and then stop. Have the children name some foods they would look for if they were very hungry. Ask, "Are these the kind of foods a caterpillar might eat?" Resume the story. After each day is mentioned in the story, have the children name the next day of the week. Let them predict some foods that the very hungry caterpillar might eat next.

6

Overview of Activities *(cont.)*

ENJOYING THE STORY

1. **Story Props.** Make the story props on pages 12 to 14. Check the children's recall and comprehension with the activities listed on page 11.

2. **Real or Make Believe.** Although *The Very Hungry Caterpillar* is based on facts, some of the story events are definitely fiction. Establish the difference between what is real and what is make believe. Make copies of the chart on page 15 and give one to each pair of children. Reread *The Very Hungry Caterpillar* to the class. Direct the children to write or draw some story events that are real and some that are make believe.

3. **Story Problems.** Combine math with writing. See page 16 for complete directions.

4. **Days of the Week.** Count to five. Then state the five school days in order (Monday...). Review what the hungry caterpillar ate each day. Let the children finish each sentence in words or pictures (see page 17).

5. **Math Matching.** Make the math game board on page 19. Let pairs of children match the set cards with their corresponding numerals on the game board. Keep the completed game boards at your math center.

6. **Story Order.** Check how well the children know the story events in *The Very Hungry Caterpillar*. Cut apart the sentence strips on page 25. Glue each sentence to a construction paper strip. Hand out the ten strips to ten children. Let the children place themselves in correct story order. Have the rest of the class read the story. To check the story order, keep *The Very Hungry Caterpillar* book handy.

7. **Creative Writing.** Encourage creative writing with any of the activities outlined on page 21. Children can complete unfinished sentences, make charts to use as word banks, create similes, or develop an innovation.

8. **Art.** Make caterpillars. See page 67 for two different art projects.

9. **Butterfly/Chrysalis Puppet Performance.** Make a butterfly/chrysalis hand puppet. Use it for a performance of the butterfly life cycle, page 11, or a retelling of *The Very Hungry Caterpillar*.

10. **Leaf Addition/Subtraction.** Show the children the back of *The Very Hungry Caterpillar* book. Have them find the small egg on the leaf. Provide each child with a piece of green construction paper. Have the children cut or tear the paper into a leaf shape. While they are doing this, provide 10 (for basic addition/subtraction) to 20 (for more complex addition/subtraction) dry white beans (which will represent the "eggs"). Share a verbal story problem while the children manipulate the "eggs" and leaves. For example, "I looked up in the tree and I saw three eggs on a leaf." (Children place three beans on their leaves.) "The next morning, I saw two more eggs on the same leaf." (Children add two more beans to the three beans on their leaves.) "How many eggs are on the leaf now?" (Children verbally share answers.) After enough modeling, allow children to work with partners to create story problems for their partners to "act out" with their beans and leaves.

Overview of Activities *(cont.)*

EXTENDING THE STORY

1. **Illustrations.** Take time to examine Eric Carle's artwork in *The Very Hungry Caterpillar*. What method do the children think Mr. Carle used to create his unusual illustrations? Explain how tissue paper collage is made. Let children make a tissue paper collage art project. See page 23 for complete directions.

2. **Life Cycles.** Learn the stages of the butterfly life cycle. Have the children make life cycle strips on page 22. Let the children practice telling the story of the life cycle to a partner.

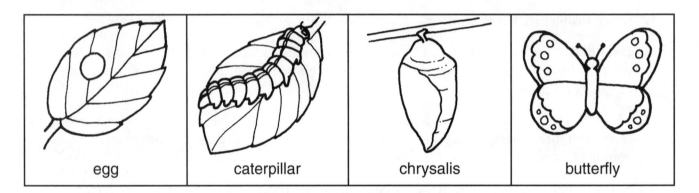

| egg | caterpillar | chrysalis | butterfly |

3. **Innovations.** Invent a new story. Change the insect from a caterpillar to a bee or an ant. See what creative situations the children can think of!

4. **More by Eric Carle.** Go to the library to find some other picture books written by Eric Carle (see the Bibliography on page 80). Let the children copy some of his other titles and choose one to check out. Read one or two of the stories to the children. Compare the illustrations in the newly-read books to the illustrations in *The Very Hungry Caterpillar*. Ask the children what art method they think was used to make the illustrations in those books. Try some of the different art mediums Eric Carle used. Note: Often there is an explanation of his art medium in the book, either on the book jacket or near the copyright information.

5. **Culminating Activity.** Make a giant caterpillar book. Enlarge the caterpillar pattern from page 14 (a method for enlargement can be found on page 24). Give each group of children a giant caterpillar. Have them look through magazines and cut out pictures of foods that a very hungry caterpillar might eat.

6. **Oops. An Honest Mistake!** Look on the page in the story where the caterpillar makes "a little brown house." It states he made a cocoon. This is scientifically incorrect. A moth emerges from a cocoon, a butterfly emerges from a chrysalis. Does Eric Carle know this? Have your children compose a class letter to mail to Mr. Carle (you can contact him through the book publisher). It will be a joy for the children when Mr. Carle responds!

About Caterpillars and Butterflies

On this page you will find some important facts for your own reference written with simple explanations so you can share these facts with your children.

1. Butterfly eggs come in many different shapes and colors. Some are hard to see because they are so small. While some eggs are round or oval, others may be shaped like cones, gumdrops, or even dill pickles. They can be green, red, blue, yellow, or brown in color.

2. An adult butterfly lays eggs which hatch into caterpillars that eventually turn themselves into butterflies. A butterfly mother always lays her eggs on a leaf that is her favorite "leaf food" so that when her eggs hatch there will be plenty of food for her babies to eat. Some butterflies lay one egg at a time, while others lay hundreds of them side by side in neat rows. Young caterpillars may hatch out of the eggs in a week or so, or the eggs may remain dormant (asleep) for months.

3. Hatched caterpillars can be found in fields, woods, parks, and gardens. They are usually found under leaves or on the branches of trees and shrubs. (Be careful when you are looking; caterpillars that have hairy bodies can be poisonous and dangerous and should not be picked up.)

4. Most caterpillars have three pairs of legs near the front of their bodies and four to six pairs near the back end of their bodies. All along the sides of their bodies are breathing holes (nine pairs). They have twelve eyes. Caterpillars' bodies are usually divided into twelve parts.

5. A caterpillar makes munching and crunching noises when it eats. Its little jaws are very strong. As a caterpillar eats, it gets too fat for its skin. While it is growing, the caterpillar will shed its skin four or five times. When it molts for the last time, the caterpillar makes a shell, called a chrysalis, around itself. While it is inside the chrysalis, the caterpillar's body is changing into a butterfly.

6. Some chrysalises are gold colored or are decorated with gold and silver spots, while others are green, purple, or gray with odd-looking bumps and spines. Incubation can be as short as two weeks, but some caterpillars do not emerge as butterflies until spring, which means they would have a much longer incubation period.

7. When the butterfly breaks open and crawls out of one end of the chrysalis, it will be damp. It will stretch out its wings to dry and after about two hours it will be ready to fly. When it is old enough, it will fly away to find a mate. The female will then lay her eggs on her favorite leafy plant. Eventually, the eggs will hatch into caterpillars, and the whole life cycle will begin again.

8. Caterpillars may not look like it, but they have a head, a thorax, and an abdomen. They also have six legs, therefore caterpillars are insects. It may look like a caterpillar has lots of legs, but they are not really legs. They are called prolegs.

9. Butterflies use camouflage to protect themselves. Some butterflies use spots on their wings, while others use certain colors to keep predators away.

10. Many species of butterflies migrate (move to where it is warmer in the winter). The Monarch butterfly often travels hundreds of miles to find warmer climates during the winter season.

Butterfly Homes

Create classroom excitement by raising your own butterflies. Classroom kits can often be purchased through local educational supply stores and catalogs (see page 77 for a listing of possible sources). But if your budget does not permit this expense you may want to build your own.

Materials

A clear plastic soda bottle, clean and dry; scissors; aluminum foil; rubber band; pencil; potting soil; a small plant (preferably a cutting from which a caterpillar has been found); water; twigs; caterpillar

Note: A clear plastic jar with a lid also works well for this project. If one is used, you will not need the scissors, aluminum foil, or rubber band.

Directions

1. Use the scissors to cut off the top portion of the bottle (see diagram). Discard this top portion.

2. Fill the bottom of the soda bottle with potting soil (about one-fourth full).

3. Plant the cutting or small plant in the soil; moisten the soil.

4. Stand up some twigs close to the leaf.

5. Place the caterpillar on a leaf of the plant.

6. Cover the top of the bottle with aluminum foil and secure with a rubber band.

7. Poke holes in the foil lid for ventilation (a pencil works well for this procedure).

8. Observe daily. Add water to the plant as needed.

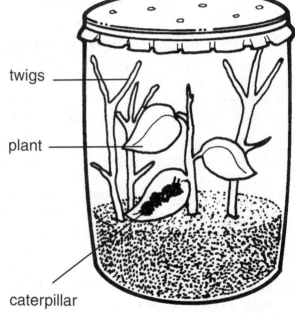

aluminum foil

twigs

plant

caterpillar

soda bottle

Follow-up Activities

1. While the caterpillar is in its chrysalis, have the children make a chrysalis of their own by wrapping twine or brown yarn around a toilet tissue roll. Each child then can make a small paper butterfly to place inside the chrysalis. The children can remove their paper butterflies when the real butterfly emerges from its chrysalis.

2. As the butterfly begins to emerge from its chrysalis, watch its wings slowly emerge and dry. Then take the butterfly outside and let it go.

3. Discuss with the children where they think the butterfly will go and what it will do now. Have them draw pictures of the butterfly's adventures.

10

Story Props

Assembling

1. Reproduce, color, cut out and glue patterns (pages 12-14) to tagboard. (Patterns may first be enlarged with an overhead projector or a copy machine with an enlargement feature, if desired.) Laminate for durability. Staple a craft stick to the bottom of each shape.

2. To use the patterns (pages 12-14) on a flannelboard, trace each pattern onto interfacing fabric (Pellon®), available at fabric stores. Color with marking pens; cut out.

Uses

1. Distribute props to the children. As you reread the story have the children who are holding the appropriate prop(s) stand up when mentioned.

2. Display story props and make up riddles about them. Example, "A caterpillar builds me around its body and stays inside until it changes into a butterfly. What am I?" (chrysalis). Call on a student to name and choose the correct prop.

Butterfly/Chrysalis Puppet Performance

Create a caterpillar/chrysalis puppet by using two pairs of sweat pants, one brown and one green (It is recommended to use old pairs or purchase used ones at a second-hand thrift store.) Cut one leg off both pairs of sweat pants at the crotch line. Put the cut brown leg (chrysalis) into the cut green leg (caterpillar) *wrong sides together.* Sew the elastic (ankle) bands of both legs together, while at the same time sewing closed the ankle openings. Sew on large google craft eyes near sewn area of the green leg's opening for the caterpillar eyes.

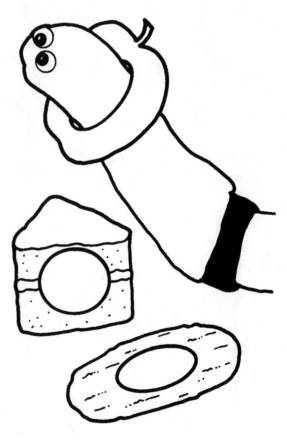

Place your arm into the puppet until it reaches the head area. With your other hand, feed the caterpillar enlarged, cut-out and laminated food items (patterns, pages 12-14) that have had a circle cut out of the center of each item to form edible food "bracelets." "Feed" the caterpillar the food props as you tell the story of *The Very Hungry Caterpillar.* After feeding the caterpillar puppet all the food "bracelets," carefully pull the bottom opening of the puppet (make certain you grab the hidden brown puppet, as well) up and over the food items until the caterpillar puppet is literally inside-out and the brown puppet (the chrysalis) "hangs" from your clenched fist. Then, when appropriate in your story telling, have a paper or material butterfly "fly out" (come out from behind the chrysalis puppet) of its little brown house.

Story Props *(cont.)*

See page 11 for suggested use.

12

Story Props *(cont.)*

See page 11 for suggested use.

Story Props *(cont.)*

See page 11 for suggested use.

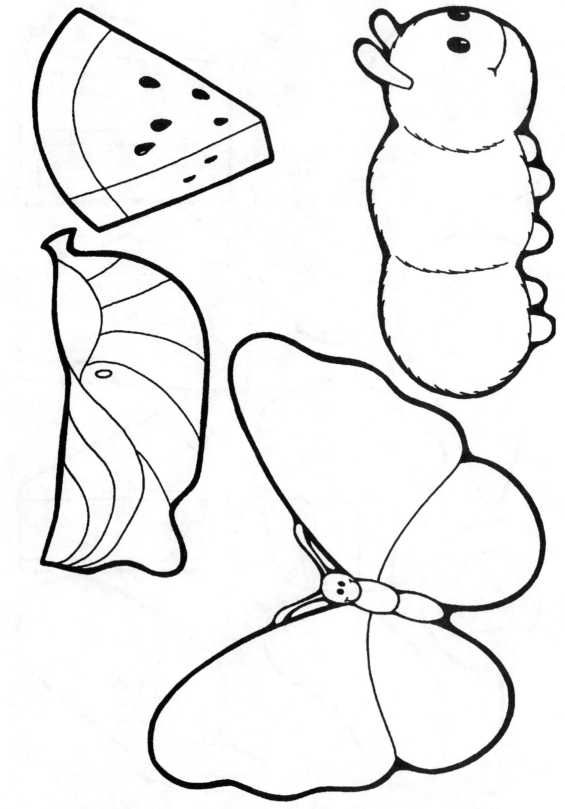

14

Real or Make Believe

Some story events in *The Very Hungry Caterpillar* are real and could happen. Some story events are make believe. Draw pictures or tell about some things that are real and some things that are make believe in *The Very Hungry Caterpillar.*

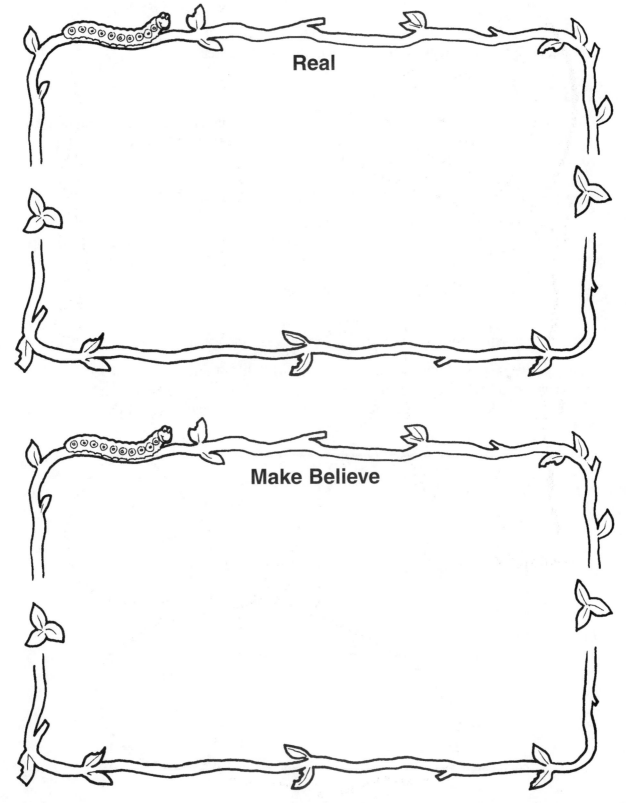

Real

Make Believe

Story Problem Book

Math and writing go hand-in-hand and this activity will show you one way you can combine the two subjects. This class project will also help the children practice their counting skills and review basic math facts.

Materials

White drawing paper; pencils; crayons; paper punch; three-ring binder

Directions

1. Have the children count the number of fruits on a given day in the story. Let the children copy or complete this sentence, "The hungry caterpillar ate _____ (number) _____ (food) on _____ (day)." A possible sentence could be written as:

"The caterpillar ate *four strawberries* on *Thursday*."

2. Give each child a sheet of drawing paper. Show the children how to fold the sheet of drawing paper in half by bringing the bottom half up to meet the top of the paper. Then turn the paper sideways.

3. Tell the children to write a word sentence on the left side of the paper (see diagram).

4. Then have the children illustrate their problems and use a paper punch to punch the corresponding number of holes near the far right edge of the paper (see diagram at right).

5. Collect all the pages and punch two holes near the top edge of each page. Make a cover for the book; punch two holes at the top edge of the cover, too. Thread some yarn or ribbon through the holes; tie with a bow. Place the completed math story problem book in your classroom library.

Counting to Five

Read what the very hungry caterpillar ate each day. Write and draw what you would like to eat on each day.

On **Monday** the very hungry caterpillar ate one apple.	On **Monday** I ate one…
On **Tuesday** the very hungry caterpillar ate two pears.	On **Tuesday** I ate two…
On **Wednesday** the very hungry caterpillar ate three plums.	On **Wednesday** I ate three…
On **Thursday** the very hungry caterpillar ate four strawberries.	On **Thursday** I ate four…
On **Friday** the very hungry caterpillar ate five oranges.	On **Friday** I ate five…

Caterpillar Facts Review

Directions

Cut out the caterpillar shape and glue to tagboard. Color and laminate for more durability. Punch holes along the perimeter of the caterpillar's body. Write a different problem next to each hole punched. Turn the caterpillar over and write the answers to the problems next to the corresponding hole. Staple two craft sticks or tongue depressors together to the bottom of the caterpillar placing one stick on each side of the caterpillar (see small diagrams above). Make several review caterpillars.

To Play

Two children can play with one caterpillar manipulative. One child faces the front of the caterpillar while the other child faces the back of the caterpillar. The child facing the front puts a pencil or golf tee through a hole and says and completes the problem aloud. The child facing the back of the caterpillar checks the answers. After all problems have been solved, the children trade places and use another caterpillar.

Extensions

This can also be adapted to simple spelling (Example: A picture of a cat on one side and the word *cat* on the other.); syllabication (Example: The word *butterfly* on one side; the numeral *3* on the other.); or other educational skills.

The Hungry Caterpillar Game

Make a game board for children to use with a partner. For each game board you will need a copy of the game pieces, below, and the gameboard, page 20, both run on card stock. Color and laminate the pages. Cut apart the game pieces. Attach a small envelope to the back of the game board. On the outside of the envelope write *Game Pieces;* add pieces and include small plastic butterflies or other objects to the envelope to use as markers. Following the directions on page 20, play the game with the children. Afterwards, place the completed game boards at a center in your classroom so the children can play on their own.

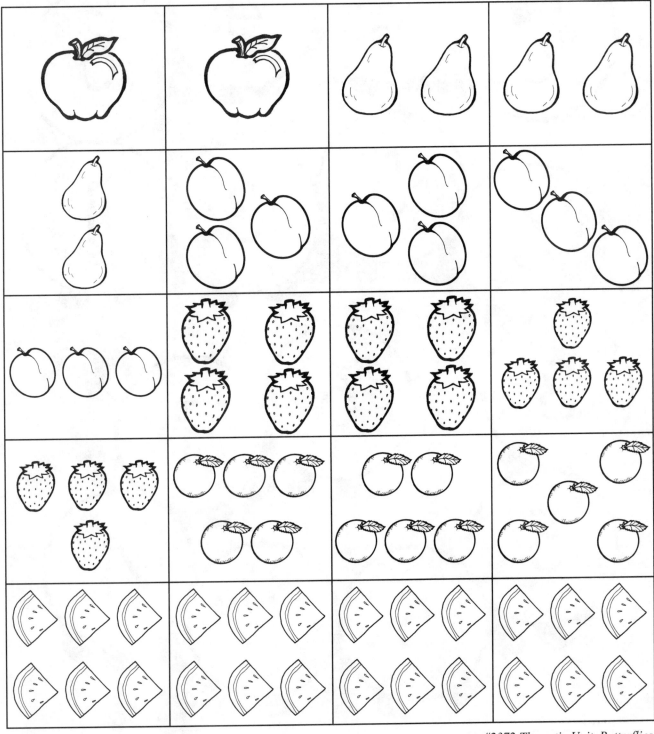

The Hungry Caterpillar Game *(cont.)*

See page 19 for suggested use.

Directions: Draw a card. Count the fruit on the card. Move your marker to the next space that has the numeral that matches the number of fruit on your card.

Creative Writing

Vibrant illustrations and simple text have made *The Very Hungry Caterpillar* one of the most endearing and popular children's stories ever written. Four creative writing ideas are explored below. The butterfly pattern on page 26 may be used with any of these activities to record the students' creative thoughts.

Writing in the Round

Give each child one paper plate and some crayons. Direct them to draw a butterfly environment (flowers, grass, trees, etc.) on the bottom half of the plate. On the top half have the children copy and finish any of these sentences, writing the sentence around the perimeter of the paper plate:

If I were inside a chrysalis . . .
If I had six legs . . .
If I could fly like a butterfly . . .

From construction paper, have each child draw a butterfly; cut out. Push a brad fastener through the top of the butterfly; pull prongs apart and flatten. Place butterfly on the paper plate. Place a strong magnet under the plate where the butterfly is sitting and move the magnet around. Watch the butterfly flutter its wings all around the plate!

Innovations

Change the main character of *The Very Hungry Caterpillar* to a very busy bee. With the class brainstorm some adventures that the bee might have. Ask the children what the bee would do on Sunday. What would it do on Monday? Continue through the days of the week, naming new activities for each day. Make separate sentence strips for each day of the week and its accompanying activities. Glue each strip to a separate sheet of paper. Give one to each group of children to illustrate. Compile all the pages together to make a classroom big book.

Similes

Discuss some likenesses between butterflies and caterpillars with the class. For example, "A butterfly is as colorful as . . ." Have the children finish the statement. They might respond with ". . . *a rainbow* or *a box of crayons.*" Direct the children to copy or write a simile, finish it, and draw a picture. Some other similes to use include:

. . . as graceful as a . . .   . . . as beautiful as a . . .   . . . as colorful as . . .

Charts

Construct a class chart of caterpillar and butterfly characteristics. For example, brainstorm ideas about *noises they make, things they do, words that describe them, where they live,* etc. Children can then incorporate some of these words and phrases in their writing. Have the children choose either the caterpillar or the butterfly to write about. Let the children tell something that the insect did and explain how or where it was. Sample sentences might be: The butterfly *flew fast.* The caterpillar *crawled* on a *tree branch.*

Butterfly Life Cycle

Eric Carle's tale of a very hungry caterpillar gives children a simplified version of the butterfly life cycle. Help children gain more understanding and knowledge of the actual process with the following activity.

Materials

Light blue construction paper cut into 3" x 18" (8 x 35 cm) strips; dried white beans; green pipe cleaners, 3" (7.5 cm) long; cotton balls; brown tempera paint powder; self-sealing plastic bag; glue; butterfly stickers or small butterfly shapes cut from paper; crayons

Directions

1. Give each child a construction paper strip.

2. Direct the children to fold the long strip in half and then in half again to create four sections. Help the children crease their folds, if necessary.

3. Have the children glue a white bean in the center of the first section. At the bottom let the children write the word *egg*. (*Optional:* Before gluing bean, use a green crayon to color a leaf in this section for the egg to "lay" on.)

4. In the second section glue on a green pipe cleaner which has been bent in a ripple fashion to resemble a caterpillar. Write the word *caterpillar*.

5. To the third section glue *prepared* cotton balls. (Preparation: Place the cotton balls in the plastic bag. Pour in a small amount of brown tempera paint *powder*, seal, and shake. The white cotton balls will turn brown.) Write the word *chrysalis*.

6. Glue the butterfly to the fourth section and write the word *butterfly*.

7. Let the children practice explaining the butterfly's life story using their completed life cycles.

Extension

Use a paper plate instead of a strip of construction paper. Divide the plate into four sections. Glue one item (white bean, green pipe cleaner, cotton ball, butterfly) to each section and label it as directed above.

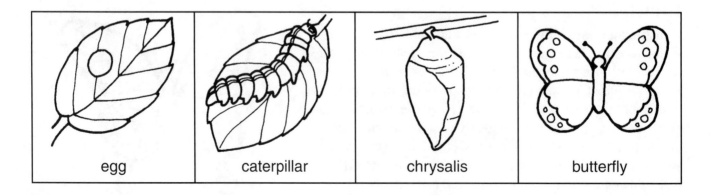

| egg | caterpillar | chrysalis | butterfly |

Tissue Paper Collage

One likely reason why *The Very Hungry Caterpillar* has become such a favorite classic among children and adults is the sumptuous artwork. When author Eric Carle employed the use of tissue paper collage to accompany the text, he revolutionized illustrations in children's books. It is difficult for anyone to resist liking the vibrant colors and delicate textures of the designs on the pages. Let children experience the tissue paper collage method that Carle has perfected in his books. All necessary supplies and directions are outlined below.

Materials

A variety of colored art tissue paper; brushes of various widths; containers (margarine tubs or yogurt cups are good to use) of thinned white glue or laundry starch (thin the glue or starch with water); scissors; pencils; white or light-colored construction paper for the background; smocks or aprons (old shirts buttoned backwards work well); newspaper to cover the working surfaces; a table or other area to dry the papers; crayons, pastels, and markers

Directions

1. Call the children's attention to the pictures in *The Very Hungry Caterpillar*. Briefly discuss how Eric Carle constructed them.

2. Cover the work surfaces with newspaper and give each child a smock to wear.

3. Give each child a sheet of construction paper and a pencil.

4. Have the children use pencils to sketch an outline of a butterfly, caterpillar, or a scene from the story. (You may want to supply young children with a prepared pattern. See page 14 or 26 for possible patterns.)

5. Have the children tear (or have them pre-torn) small pieces of the colored art tissue.

6. Overlap the tissue pieces inside the outline of the sketched butterfly, caterpillar or scene.

7. Brush the top surfaces of the torn tissue with the thinned glue or starch.

8. Encourage the children to experiment with colors. Subtle shadings can be obtained by overlapping pieces of the same color while brilliant combinations and contrasts appear when different colors overlap.

9. Allow the art tissue collages to dry thoroughly.

10. Have the children add details and textures to their collages with crayons, pastels, and markers; display.

Giant Caterpillar Book

An excellent culminating project for a thematic unit is the making of classroom books.

Materials

A caterpillar pattern (suggested pattern, see page 14); transparency sheet and pen; an overhead projector; black marking pen; scissors; butcher paper; and masking tape

Directions

1. Place the transparency sheet over the caterpillar pattern.

2. Trace the outline of the caterpillar onto the transparency sheet using a transparency marker. Place the transparency on the overhead projector.

3. Secure a large sheet of butcher paper to a chalkboard or bulletin board with the masking tape.

4. Project the caterpillar image onto the butcher paper and trace the outline with a thick-tipped black marking pen.

5. Cut out the enlarged caterpillar and repeat method to make as many caterpillar "pages" as needed.

Activities

1. **Hungry Caterpillar.** Have a supply of old magazines available. Give each group of two to three children a large caterpillar page, scissors, and glue. Direct the children to look through the magazines to find and cut out pictures of foods that a very hungry caterpillar might eat. Have them then glue the pictures to the caterpillar's body. Collect all the pages, add a cover page, and create a big book.

2. **Rewrite.** Rewrite *The Very Hungry Caterpillar* using the foods that children have glued to their caterpillar pages, as directed in activity one. Another rewriting idea can be done by retelling the story using another main character (i.e. ant, bee, dragonfly) eating different food items.

3. **Sentence Strip Big Book.** Make ten large caterpillars as directed above. Reproduce the sentence strips on page 25; cut apart. Glue one sentence onto each giant caterpillar page. Give one caterpillar to each group of children to illustrate. Attach the caterpillars to the wall in correct story order. Let the children read the wall. After displaying the caterpillars for a while, remove from the wall and bind the pages into a big book by stacking the pages in sequential order. Add a front and back cover and bind.

24

Sentence Strips

See page 24 for suggested use.

He ate five oranges on Friday.
On Monday he ate one apple.
A tiny caterpillar hatched out of the egg.
A beautiful butterfly emerged from the chrysalis.
On Thursday he ate four strawberries.
He began to look for food.
Wednesday he ate three plums.
He got a stomachache on Saturday.
He ate two pears on Tuesday.
The caterpillar built a chrysalis.

Butterfly Pattern

Suggested Uses: art projects; creative writing; stationery to send notes home

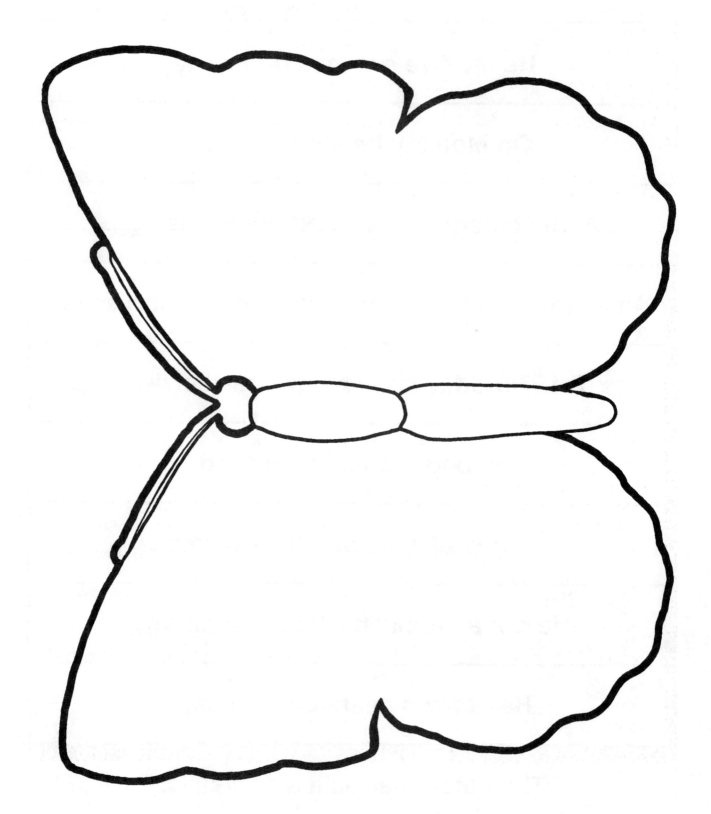

26

Where Butterflies Grow

by Joanne Ryder

Summary

In a green growing place, a wonderful transformation is about to take place. From a tiny egg underneath a leaf emerges a thin, dark, creeping caterpillar. As it begins to grow it eats and eats until its skin feels tight. After shedding this skin the caterpillar continues to eat and grow some more. Soon it is time for the caterpillar to hunt for a place that can offer it protection from its enemies. As it stretches out of its old skin, a new temporary home is formed around its body. Inside the chrysalis amazing changes are beginning to take place. When it is ready, a fully-formed butterfly emerges from within the dark home. At first it is wet and crumpled but soon its wings unfold and dry. The butterfly slowly spreads its wings and flies off to eat and find others like itself.

The outline below is a suggested plan for using the various activities that are presented in this unit. You should adapt these ideas to fit your own classroom situation.

Sample Plan

Lesson 1

- Make a prediction display board (page 28, #2) and read *Where Butterflies Grow*.

- Begin the Food Experiences (page 39).

Lesson 2

- Review the story events, then make a Chain of Events (page 31).

- Create a list of word opposites from the story and use them in a creative writing activity (page 33).

- Play a matching game (page 33).

- Pick out position phrases from the book. Have the children write sentences (page 30).

Lesson 3

- Complete the Before and After activity (page 35), matching unprepared food with prepared food.

- Relive the butterfly life cycle using the Storyboard activity on page 32.

- Make caterpillar and butterfly masks (page 37).

- Use the reading strategies on page 30 to enhance and expand reading and vocabulary skills.

Lesson 4

- Coutinue the Food Experiences (page 39).

- Make egg carton caterpillars (page 38).

- Learn more about caterpillars (pages 41 and 42).

Lesson 5

- For a Culminating Activity review the butterfly life cycle by making a shape book (pages 45 and 46).

- Complete the Extension Activity: Two Butterfly Tales (page 47).

Overview of Activities

SETTING THE STAGE

1. Set the mood for the story *Where Butterflies Grow* with a number of flower-decorated umbrellas that simulate a butterfly garden. Make the flowers out of construction paper, or use imitation flowers, and attach them to the open canopies of the umbrella. Set up the open umbrellas on the floor around the room and let the children sit under or among them while you read the story aloud.

2. Construct a portable display board to introduce the story *Where Butterflies Grow*. Attach three sections of poster board (available at art supply and teacher supply stores) together with masking tape (or purchase a science display board). Label the left section *Predictions;* label the right section *Story Events*. Make a large leaf out of green construction paper and attach to the center section, securing only the top section of the leaf to the background. Above the leaf make letters to spell out the title, "Lift up a leaf and imagine…" (See diagram at

    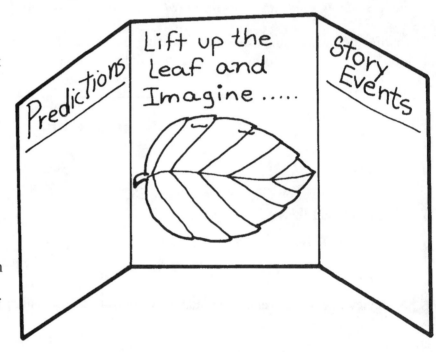

    right.) Prepare the following paper props to fit underneath the leaf: a tiny egg, a caterpillar, a chrysalis, and a butterfly (patterns for the latter three can be found on pages 12 to 14). Show the children the portable display board and read the title. Without lifting up the leaf, ask the children what they think will be underneath it (you will have taped the tiny egg underneath the leaf before showing the children the display board). Write their predictions in the left section of the display board. After you have read the story to the point of the tiny egg's introduction, lift up the green leaf on the display board to reveal the egg. Ask the children to hide their eyes while you replace the tiny egg with the next item they will be listening for in the story. Allow them to make predictions, then continue reading. Continue this process for the chrysalis and the butterfly, as well. After you have finished the entire story, use the right side of the display board to review with the children the names of the items found underneath the leaf (as well as in the story) and the sequential process of the story's events.

3. Show the illustrations throughout the story *Where Butterflies Grow*. Ask the children if they can tell what the story will be about from what the illustrations are showing. After you have looked at all of the illustrations, read the story to the children to find out what the story is actually about.

Overview of Activities *(cont.)*

ENJOYING THE BOOK

1. Review the story events with the whole group. Then let the children construct their own Chain of Events (see page 31). Cut out each strip and connect them to make a paper chain. An alternative activity is the storyboard project on page 32.

2. Find pairs of opposites within the text of *Where Butterflies Grow*. Make opposite cards (see pages 33 and 34) and play a matching game with the children. More language opportunities can be found on page 33.

3. Make caterpillar and butterfly face masks and use them for dramatic play activities. See page 37.

4. Sample some Food Experiences. A different recipe for each day of the school week can be found on page 39.

5. Learn about a butterfly's body parts. For homework, children can review what they have learned with the worksheet, Butterfly Body Parts, found on page 44.

6. Find out more about caterpillars with the following directions activity on pages 41 and 42.

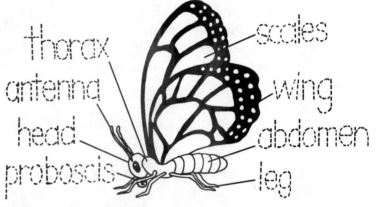

EXTENDING THE BOOK

1. Identify the other animals that are depicted in the book. Find out the names of some of the flowers that are illustrated on the pages of *Where Butterflies Grow*. (The names of flowers that butterflies like can be found on page 57.)

2. Complete the Why is a Butterfly an Insect? activity on page 43.

3. Find out about moths (see the Bibliography on page 79). Compare them with butterflies in a Venn diagram, noting the similarities and the differences. (TCM 2371—*Silkworms and Mealworms* is a great resource for learning about silkworm moths and moths in general.)

4. Complete a chart comparing the book *Where Butterflies Grow* with *The Very Hungry Caterpillar*. A prepared chart, Two Butterfly Tales, can be found on page 47.

5. Review the butterfly life cycle by making a jumbo shape book. See the directions on page 45 to 46.

6. Engage the children in an active movement experience by looking through *Where Butterflies Grow* for all the active verbs (see suggestions under "Enactment," page 30). Read the text aloud as the children physically act out the verbs, or challenge them to make new sentences that they can act out.

Reading Strategies

On this page you will find a number of learning strategies designed to help the children develop and expand their reading and vocabulary skills. Use those activities which best match your teaching style and/or modify the activities to suit your class' skill needs.

Letter Configuration

Choose a number of words from the text of the story that you want to introduce or reinforce. Write each one on a separate index card. Make a separate outline of each word on another index card, as shown in the figure at right. Let the children match the words with their configurations. After you have worked with the words for some time show the children the configurations only. Have them name the correct word. Extend the activity by asking the children to name other words that might fit with a given configuration. (For example: *tree* will have the same configuration as *have*; *bug* the same configuration as *tap*.)

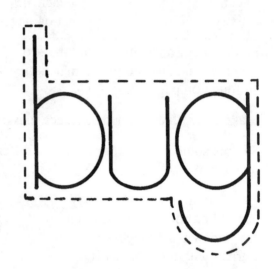

Enactment

As you read the book *Where Butterflies Grow* make a note of the action verbs. Next, copy the verbs in context sentences. For example, "You *swallow* air *puffing* up and up till your tight skin *splits*." "Then you *curl* and *stretch* till your old skin *splits* loose." "You *wiggle, shaking* your striped skin down and down till it *falls* away." Read aloud these sentences and have the children physically act out the actions.

Position Phrases

Reread *Where Butterflies Grow* to find some phrases that show position. Mark these phrases with sticky notes. Some positional phrases include *up* the stems, *underneath* the leaf, and *above* the flowers. Read these phrases aloud and direct the children to choose one to write and/or illustrate.

Extension: Extend the positional phrase activity, above, with expanded sentences. Ask the children what went up the stem or what flew above the flowers. Write sentences that incorporate these phrases. You may want to use these phrases and other words to make word or sentence cards for use with a pocket chart.

30

Chain of Events

These sentences can be used to review the story events in the book *Where Butterflies Grow*. Give each child a sentence that has been copied onto a strip of construction paper; have each child illustrate the sentence on the back side of the strip, if desired. Staple or glue the eight sequential sentences together to form a traditional paper chain link.

1. A caterpillar bursts out of the egg.

2. The caterpillar eats and eats.

3. The caterpillar's skin gets tight. It falls off.

4. Every day the caterpillar eats and grows.

5. One day the caterpillar makes a silken sling.

6. Inside, the caterpillar is changing.

7. A wet butterfly crawls out of the chrysalis.

8. The butterfly dries its wings and flies away.

Storyboard

A storyboard is a pictorial of the major events of a story in sequence. After you have read and enjoyed the story a number of times, the children will be ready to make one. Completed in cooperative groups, the storyboard begins with a whole class discussion. Follow the directions below to create a storyboard for *Where Butterflies Grow*.

Materials

Long sheets of white butcher paper, one for each group; masking tape; crayons; colored markers, or tempera paints and brushes

Directions

1. Prepare for this activity by taping the butcher paper to a long table, the classroom floor, or a chalkboard so that the children will have easy access to it.

2. Assemble the whole class and ask them to recall the major events of the story. Record the events on chart paper in written form and with simple illustrations.

3. Ask the children which event came first, second, etc., until all events have been accounted for. Make sure that the children are clear on the correct story order. Number the events on the chart paper, if necessary.

4. Divide the children into small cooperative groups of three or four.

5. Explain that each group will be making their own story map of the important events in the story *Where Butterflies Grow*.

6. Direct the groups to begin their story maps from the left side edge of the butcher paper.

7. After they have illustrated the first story event they continue in the same manner until the story has been completely mapped out. Challenge them to write a sentence or sentences for each of their story events.

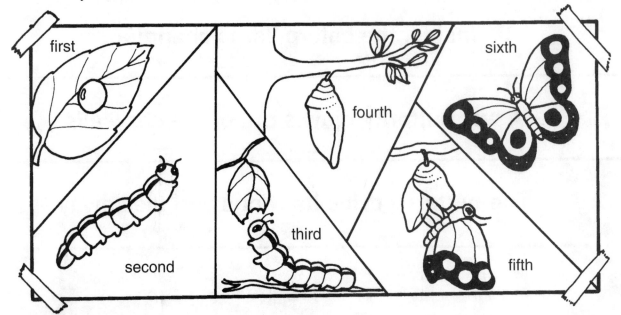

Language Arts

Encourage language development and creative writing with any of these activities. Adapt them to suit your teaching style and classroom needs. Some of these exercises may be completed orally rather than written, if preferred.

Imagine…

Reread the first page of *Where Butterflies Grow*. Stop after the last sentence, "Lift up a leaf and imagine…" Call on some children to finish the sentence. Let them copy the sentence and draw/write an ending for it under a piece of green construction paper cut in the shape of a leaf and stapled to the end of a sentence strip.

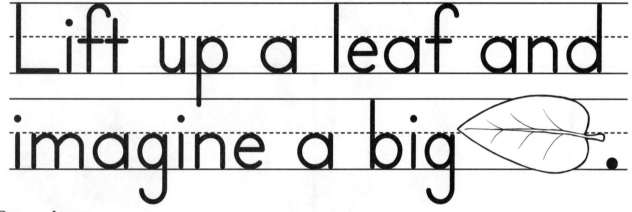

Opposites

There are plenty of words in the story that have opposites (see the sample list below). Read a sentence from the story text that contains one of these words. Call attention to the word and ask the children if they can name an opposite of that word. After completing this part of the exercise, rewrite a simplified version of *Where Butterflies Grow* using opposites wherever possible.

(Words from the Story)	(Suggested Opposites)
warm	cool
bright	dark
soft	hard
tiny	large
wide	narrow
sweet	sour

Matching Game

Make copies of page 34 so that you have enough sets of this cooperative activity. Cut apart the cards along the bold lines. Place each set in an envelope. Give each pair or group of children a set of these cards. Direct the groups to match up the opposites.

These cards can also be used in your classroom pocket chart or on a flannel board. To use with a flannel board, cut strips of flannel or sandpaper. Glue one cut strip of flannel or sandpaper to the back of each card. The cards will now stick to the flannel board. (For more durability, you may want to glue the cut out words to index cards or construction paper strips and laminate them. Then attach the flannel or sandpaper strips to the back of each card.)

Language Arts *(cont.)*

See page 33 for directions.

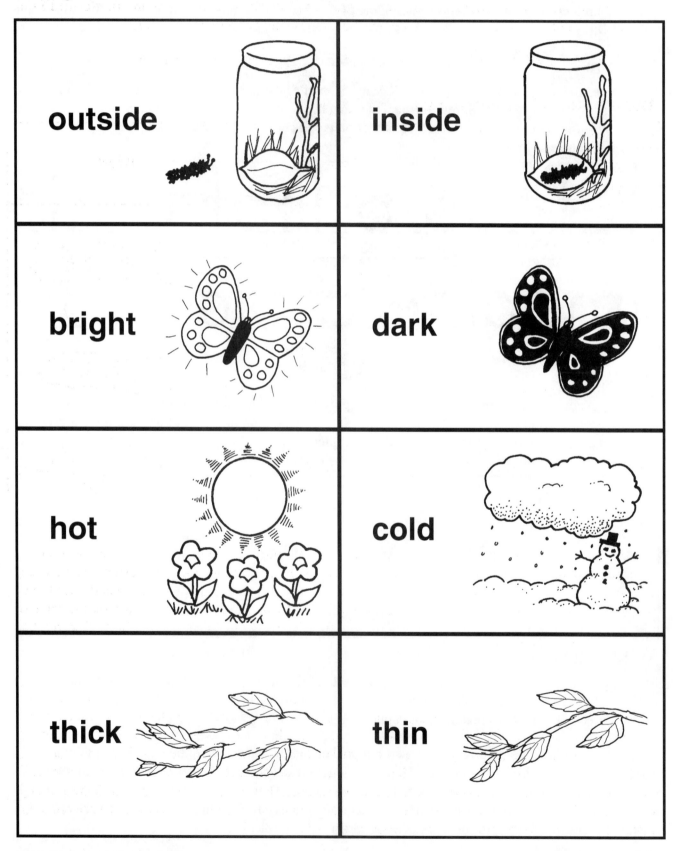

outside

inside

bright

dark

hot

cold

thick

thin

Before and After

A unit of studies about caterpillars and butterflies affords an opportune time to teach the concept of *before* and *after*. Just as caterpillars are transformed into butterflies, many foods are transformed from one form to another and can be used to demonstrate the concept of *before* and *after*.

On this page you will find three methods for reinforcing and extending this concept.

Before and After Drawings

Discuss the concept of *before* and *after* with the children. Ask them to name some examples. Use reproduced puzzle pieces (page 36) to reinforce the concept. Direct the children to draw a picture that shows *before* and *after*. Give each child a sheet of construction paper and some crayons. Show them how to fold the paper in half. Tell them to write *before* on the left side and *after* on the right side. Instruct the children to draw an appropriate picture in each section of the paper. Let them share their finished pictures with a partner or the class; display.

Before	After

Cooking

Prepare any of the following food items with the class: pop popcorn, cook rice, bake bread or biscuits (use frozen dough or canned products), make applesauce, melt ice, make flavored gelatin; bake a cake or cookies (from scratch or use a mix). Stress the concepts of *before* and *after* prior to and after food preparation. Discuss the changes that have taken place. Ask the children if the foods look the same or different after they have been prepared. Extend the activity with a *before* and *after* chart. Construct a class chart with additional pictures and/or words.

Matching

Before you begin this activity you will have to have gathered real food items in their *before* state. For example, assemble unpopped popcorn, cookie or bread dough, uncooked rice, apples, fruits, and other foods on a special table in the classroom. (If you prefer, draw pictures of these food items on index cards or sheets of construction paper.) Have the children cut out magazine pictures or draw pictures of the following food items: popcorn, cookies, cooked rice, bread, cake, applesauce, jams or jellies, or any of the other foods you have predetermined. After the pictures have been cut out/drawn, let the children match the pictures of the prepared (*after*) foods to the *before* food items.

Before and After *(cont.)*

Reproduce the puzzle pieces onto heavy cardstock. Cut apart the puzzle pieces and laminate. See page 35 for suggested use.

Caterpillar and Butterfly Faces

Make these clever caterpillar and butterfly faces to use as props in dramatic play activities or just for fun.

Materials

Empty cereal or cracker boxes; scissors; construction paper; tape; glue; yarn or string; pencil; pen; hole punch; an assortment of materials such as chenille sticks, colored plastic wrap, aluminum foil, jar lids, egg cartons, party favors

Note: An adult should help the children make the eye and mouth holes. Be sure that the mask is away from the child's face before poking eye holes.

Directions

1. Cut and save the two large front and back panels on the cereal or cracker boxes. (Each box will yield two masks.)

2. Cut each panel into an oval or rounded shape (see diagrams).

3. Cut out construction paper to match the shape of the mask; glue the construction paper to the cardboard mask.

4. Determine where the eyeholes should be by placing the mask in front of the child's face. With a pencil lightly mark the eyeholes. Making sure the mask is away from the child's face, poke the eyeholes with a pen or the scissors and cut out.

5. Hold the mask up to the child's face again and lightly mark the area where the mouth will go; cut out a mouth hole.

6. Have the children decorate the face masks with construction paper, egg carton sections, or any other available materials.

7. Punch a hole on each side of the mask (again, do this away from the child's face).

8. Thread 12" (30 cm) of yarn through each hole and tie the two pieces together at the back of the child's head.

Activities

1. As you review the life cycle of the butterfly, those children with caterpillar masks can enact the caterpillar parts—hatching from the egg, crawling along, eating a leaf, shedding, building a chrysalis. Those with butterfly parts can emerge from the chrysalis and fly away.

2. Conduct a butterfly parade. Sing butterfly songs (see page 65) and march around the room.

3. Have the children role play the life of a caterpillar and a butterfly by creating an ad-lib play or making up a pre-determined dialogue

Caterpillar Art

No lesson on caterpillars would be complete without making an egg carton caterpillar. To fill your classroom with these creepy crawlers, follow the directions below.

Note: Since this tends to be a messy project you may want to enlist help from parents. Send a note home ahead of time asking for volunteers. You may want to use the butterfly pattern on page 26 as stationery. Also ask the parents to send old shirts or smocks if you do not already have some available.

Materials

Old newspapers; tempera paint; paintbrushes; scissors; cardboard egg cartons (1 egg carton per 4 students); chenille sticks (2 halves and 6 thirds per child); old shirts or smocks; clear or masking tape

Directions

1. Prepare the egg cartons ahead of time by cutting off the tops of the egg cartons; discard. Cut each bottom portion in half lengthwise and widthwise so that you have sections of four rows with three cups each.

2. Cover the working area with newspaper. Have the children put on their smocks. Give each child a three-cup section. Tell the children to turn their sections upside down so that the hollows of the cups cannot be seen. Point out that these are the caterpillars' bodies.

3. Let each child paint his or her caterpillar's body; allow the paint to dry.

4. Poke a small hole in each side of the three body sections for the legs and two holes at the top of the front section for the antennae. Give each child the six pieces [cut in thirds] of chenille stick for the legs and the two cut halves for the antenna; insert in appropriate holes. To hold the chenille sticks in place, insert each piece far enough through the hole that the end of it can be bent downwards inside the cup. To better secure the antennae and legs, you may want to place a small piece of tape over the ends of the bent chenille sticks.

5. Let each child paint on additional features (eyes, face, etc.); allow to dry and display (or use as a part of the culminating activity described on page 74).

Food Experiences

Provide the children with a variety of food experiences. Here are one school week's worth of ideas for you to use. To make these projects even more fun, include the children in the preparation of these tasty treats. (Beware, the children should also participate in the cleanup, as well.)

Veggie Caterpillars

Alternate cherry tomatoes with zucchini slices to create a caterpillar; connect the pieces with toothpicks. Poke two holes in the cherry tomato "head" and insert two chow mein noodles for the antennae.

Fuzzy Caterpillars

Soften 8 oz. (2.25 g) of cream cheese and 12 oz. (340 g) of shredded American cheese. Blend the two cheeses together well. After the children have washed their hands, let each child make five small round balls and roll the balls in parsley flakes. Have the child arrange the balls in a caterpillar shape on a lettuce leaf. Add pimento pieces for the eyes and nose; pretzel sticks can be used for antennae.

Chrysalis Treasures

Use refrigerated biscuit dough and any type of chunk cheese to make these treats. Place a chunk of cheese in the center of a biscuit and fold the dough over onto itself. Seal the edges by crimping with a fork and bake as directed. When the children bite into their "chrysalises" a cheesy surprise will greet them!

Butterfly Salad

Slice canned peach or pear halves in half. Arrange two peach or pear halves back to back on a lettuce leaf to resemble a butterfly's wings. In between the wings, shape a small amount of cottage cheese into a butterfly's body. Add thin red licorice strips for antennae and small cherry pieces for eyes.

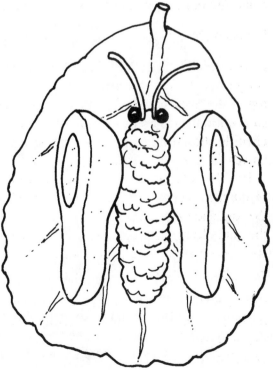

Buttery Foods

Give children the experience of trying foods with the word *butter* in them. Some foods to include could be peanut butter, apple butter, buttermilk, butter-flavored crackers, butterscotch pudding, and butter cookies.

What is a Caterpillar?

Like butterflies, caterpillars are classified as insects. Caterpillars have a head, a thorax, and an abdomen. Like other insects, caterpillars have six legs. Caterpillars have special body parts called prolegs that look like legs. Their bodies are usually furry and are divided into twelve parts, not counting the head. The children can learn more about caterpillars through any of these activities.

Pictures

Show the children pictures of a variety of caterpillars. (See the Bibliography, page 79, for helpful books with colorful illustrations.) Explain that a butterfly begins its life first as an egg and then hatches into a caterpillar, which will eventually turn into a butterfly.

Terrariums

Prepare a terrarium for house caterpillars (see page 10). Make certain that the soil is moist and there is plenty of air for the caterpillars.

Real Caterpillars

If possible, go on a nature walk to look for caterpillars. (If this is not possible, caterpillars may be ordered—see the resources on page 77.) Let the children carefully hold the caterpillars and study how they look. Observe the caterpillars under a magnifying glass (see page 63 to learn how to make a homemade magnifier). Place the caterpillars in the prepared terrarium.

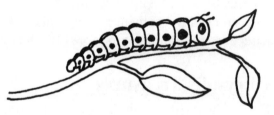

Chrysalis

After shedding their skin several times, caterpillars begin to spin a cocoon called a chrysalis. Some chrysalises are gold or are decorated with gold and silver spots. Others are green, purple, or gray with odd-looking bumps and spines. Try to locate real chrysalises for the children to observe. A great resource is a local museum or university that has an entomology program.

Entomologist

Invite a guest speaker to come to your classroom (or take a field trip). Hopefully, the speaker will be able to show real caterpillars or have great stories to tell, plus lots of interesting photographs and/or illustrations.

Faux Caterpillars

Make imitation caterpillars out of tiny green-colored marshmallows. You will need toothpicks, pipe cleaners, thin permanent markers, one large tree limb, and a container of sand to stick the tree limb in so that the limb will stand by itself. Attach several green marshmallows to a toothpick so that the toothpick is "hidden" in the marshmallows. Draw on eyes with a marker. Cut two small sections from a pipe cleaner and poke them into the head to make antennae. Attach the caterpillars to the tree limb with some glue. Display the tree limb in a special area in the classroom.

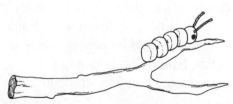

40

Caterpillar Parts

Give a child a copy of page 42 and some crayons. Tell the children to follow the directions that you are going to read to them. Show them a complete picture you have made based on the directions. Have the children check drawings for accuracy.

Read-Aloud Directions

1. **A caterpillar has six eyes on each side of its head. Draw five more small eyes in the first section near the front of your caterpillar.**

2. **Caterpillars have 12 sections. Write the numbers from one to twelve, one number in each section, starting with number one after the head. (Do not count where the eyes are!)**

3. **A caterpillar has legs and prolegs. Color all of the real legs black. They are near the front of the caterpillar's body.**

4. **A caterpillar is furry. Draw some fur along the top of your caterpillar's body with a brown crayon (the top of the body is the area that looks like it is the caterpillar's back).**

5. **Some caterpillars have black and yellow stripes as a warning to birds that they are poisonous. Make black and yellow stripes on your caterpillar's body.**

6. **Draw a leaf under your caterpillar. Make the leaf look as if your caterpillar has been eating it.**

7. **Write your name near the front end of your caterpillar's body.**

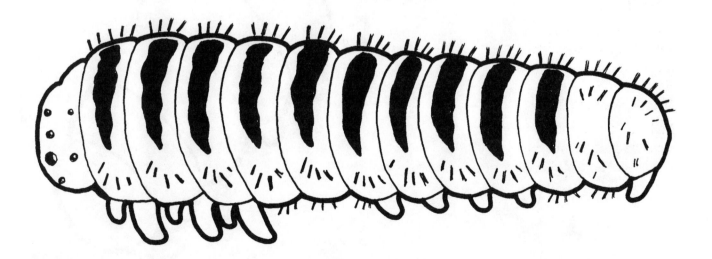

Caterpillar Parts *(cont.)*

See page 41 for suggested use.

Name_____

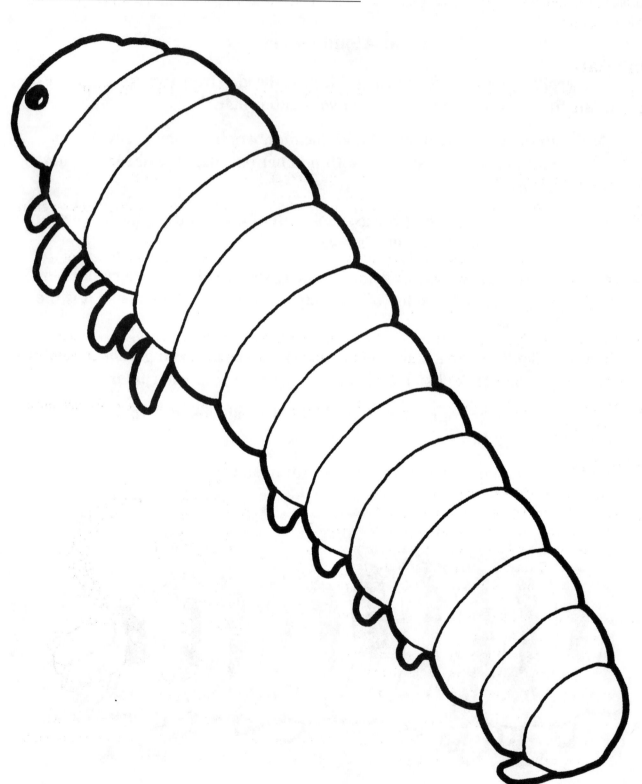

42

Why Is a Butterfly an Insect?

As you explore the topic of butterflies, some children may be curious and ask why the butterfly is an insect. It certainly doesn't look much like an ant or a beetle, yet the butterfly does resemble a mosquito or a fly in a number of ways. Explain and show the children why the butterfly is classified as an insect with this lesson.

Materials

Pictures of a butterfly and other insects (moth, ant, mosquito, fly, honeybee, dragonfly, wasp, ladybug, etc.)

Directions

1. Display some pictures of other insects. Tell the children to observe the insects.

2. Ask the children to name some ways in which the insects are alike. List their responses on chart paper.

3. Establish that an insect has three body parts—head, thorax, and abdomen—two feelers or antennae, and six legs. Some insects have wings.

4. Name and count the body parts in each insect picture.

5. Immediately after counting the parts of each insect, ask the children if that bug is an insect. Create two piles: Insect/Not An Insect. Each time it is an insect, establish that it is because it has three body parts, two feelers, and six legs.

6. Display a picture of a butterfly. Identify its insect parts—head, thorax, abdomen, two antennae, and six legs.

Extensions

1. Show the children some pictures of creepy crawlies that may or may not be insects (spiders, worms, etc.). As you display each picture have the children explain why that particular creepy crawly is or is not an insect. Make a class chart of the ones that are insects and those that are not insects.

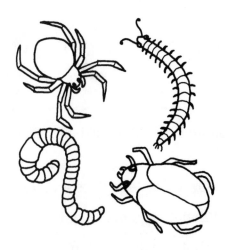

2. Learn about the internal organs of a butterfly. An excellent resource is the book *What's Inside? Insects* by Angela Royston (Dorling Kidersley, 1992). Simplified diagrams show the inner workings of the butterfly and other insects.

3. Draw a butterfly on chart paper or the chalkboard (you may wnt to use page 26 as a model). Leave off two legs, one feeler, and a wing. Call on various children to tell you what is missing. Let them draw the missing body part; repeat with different body parts missing.

4. Assign the Body Parts worksheet on page 44 for homework. Parents and guardians can work with their children to review what the children learned about butterflies.

Butterfly Body Parts

Directions

Trace the special dashed words and color the butterfly.

- -

Did you know...

two ***antennae*** or feelers on top of its ***head*** help a butterfly touch and smell?

tiny ***scales*** make the color in a butterfly's wings?

wings help a butterfly flutter gracefully in the air?

a butterfly sucks nectar through a tube or ***proboscis***?

six ***legs*** can be found on the ***thorax*** or middle section?

the stomach can be found inside a butterfly's ***abdomen***?

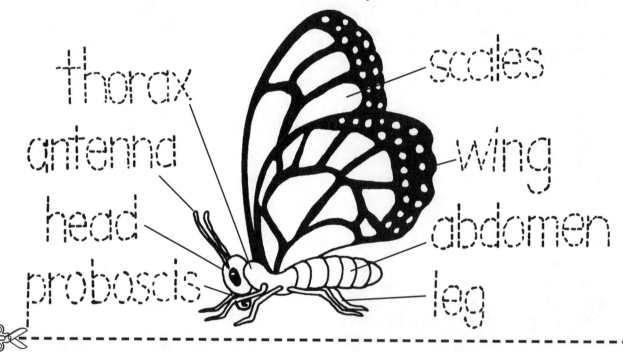

- -

Cut off and ask your child these questions: (Answers have been provided in parentheses for easy reference.)

1. How many legs does a butterfly have? (six)

2. What makes the color in a butterfly's wings? (scales)

3. What does the butterfly use to drink nectar? (proboscis or mouth)

4. In which section of the butterfly can the stomach be found? (abdomen)

5. What body part helps the butterfly fly? (wings)

6. Which body part is used to touch and smell? (antennae)

Life Cycle Shape Book

Materials

Butterfly template (see below) on page 26; cardboard; large pieces of construction paper; pencil; writing paper; copies of page 46; scissors; glue; crayons or colored markers; stapler

To Make Template

Enlarge the butterfly pattern from page 26 to desired size using a copying machine with enlarging feature (see directions below before copying). Glue enlarged butterfly pattern to cardboard; cut out silhouette. Use this as a template to make as many butterfly-shaped construction paper book pages as needed (four per child). Simply place the cardboard template onto a piece of construction paper and trace around shape with a pencil. Remove template; cut out shape.

Directions

1. Give four butterfly-shaped pages to each child; allow the child to color the butterflies.

2. Fold a sheet of writing paper into fourths; cut out the four rectangles (make sure the rectangles will fit within the butterfly shape). Give one set of four rectangles to each child. Have the child glue one rectangular sheet onto the middle area of each butterfly page.

3. Give each child a copy of page 46. Read the text together to review the main events in the life cycle of the butterfly. Tell the children to cut out the pictures on the dark lines, color the pictures and glue the pictures (one per page) sequentially onto their four butterfly pages (placing the main event picture in the center of the writing paper). Stack the pages in the correct story order; staple the pages together to form a shape book.

4. Direct the children to create a title and write it above the first illustration (see below). Then have the children write something special they have learned about each stage of a butterfly's life cycle on each page (corresponding to that page's illustration). Have the children read their completed shape books to a partner before taking the shape book home.

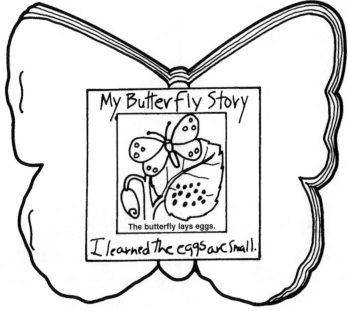

My Butterfly Story

The butterfly lays eggs.

I learned the eggs are small.

Life Cycle Shape Book *(cont.)*

See page 45 for suggested use.

The butterfly lays eggs.	**A caterpillar hatches from the egg.**
The caterpillar wraps itself in a chrysalis.	**An adult butterfly emerges.**

Two Butterfly Tales

In this book-sharing strategy, the children will be comparing the similarities and the differences between two stories: *The Very Hungry Caterpillar* and *Where Butterflies Grow*. Make a transparency of this page for the overhead projector or copy the comparison chart below onto the chalkboard or chart paper. Discuss each statement with the children and let them decide if the idea or event happened in one, the other, or both stories. Mark the appropriate columns with a check mark. For older children, make copies of the chart and let cooperative groups work together to complete the chart. You may want to ask the children to support their answers with evidence from the story.

Story Events	*The Very Hungry Caterpillar*	*Where Butterflies Grow*	Both
a caterpillar rests			
a caterpillar puffs up			
the story begins in the moonlight			
a caterpillar eats a cupcake			
an egg is on a leaf			
a caterpillar grows			
the butterfly sips nectar			
flowers are spread like umbrellas			
a caterpillar eats a leaf			
two children look under a leaf			

Circle Time

On this page you will find language activities appropriate for circle time.

Memory Game

Have the children sit in a circle. Start by telling the children that they are going to tell a new very hungry caterpillar story. Begin, "The hungry caterpillar started to look for some food. The hungry caterpillar ate *one* _____ ." Have the first child finish this sentence. The next child then says, "The hungry caterpillar ate *two* _____ ." Continue until all the children have had a turn.

Extend the activity by having the children draw a picture of everything they can remember that this new caterpillar ate. The child who draws the most correctly remembered items wins the memory game.

Another extension: Play game in the same format described above, but this time each child must repeat the prior items before adding his/her own.

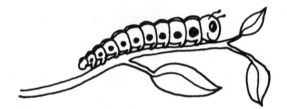

"The hungry caterpillar ate **one** apple, **two** bananas, **three** hamburgers, and **four** pizzas."

My Butterfly

Go around the circle and have each child begin a sentence with, "My butterfly has a _____ " and finishing the sentence with a word that begins with the *letter b*. Another circle time, say sentences that contain the same sound as the *beginning sound* of the word *caterpillar*. Extend this activity by naming a caterpillar- or butterfly-related word. Ask the children to name other words that begin with, or end with, the same sound as the shared word.

The Importance of Butterflies

Read aloud *The Important Book* by Margaret Wise Brown (Harper & Row, 1949). Ask the children to share reasons why they think caterpillars and butterflies are important. Follow up with a written assignment. Have the children copy the statements and complete with their thoughts:

The important thing about a caterpillar is _____ .

The important thing about a butterfly is _____ .

Let the children then illustrate their sentences.

Chants

Share the book *In the Tall, Tall Grass* by Denise Fleming (Henry Holt and Company, 1991) with the class. Reread the section that says, "…crunch, munch, caterpillar lunch." Have the children chant these words together. Make up new verses to chant.

Poetry Pages

Nature—and anything that occurs in nature—is a popular subject for poets. Butterflies and caterpillars are no exception. On this page you will find two poems to use with the children along with additional resources for butterfly and caterpillar poems. Turn to page 50 for some ideas that will inspire children to write their own poetry.

Caterpillar

Caterpillar, caterpillar, brown and furry,
Winter is coming and you'd better hurry.
Find a leaf under which to creep.
Spin a chrysalis in which to sleep.
Then when springtime comes one day,
You'll be a butterfly and fly away!

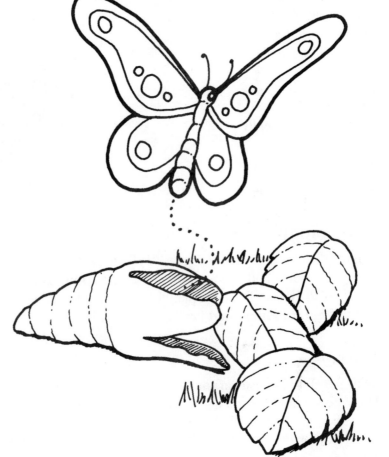

Butterfly, Butterfly

by Jan Warren

Butterfly, butterfly, laying lots of eggs.
The eggs hatch caterpillars with short, stubby legs.
Caterpillar, caterpillar, eating 'til you're big.
Then walking very slowly you hang from a twig.
Sleep now, and change, but very, very soon…
Caterpillar, caterpillar, you changed, you didn't die.
You grew wings, and long legs, to become a beautiful butterfly!

Suggested Poetry Anthologies

"The Butterfly Jar" by Jeffrey Moss, ***The Butterfly Jar*** by Jeffrey Moss (1989).

"The Caterpillar" by Christina Rosetti, ***Sing a Song of Popcorn.*** (Scholastic, 1988).

"Fuzzy Wuzzy, Creepy Crawly" by Lillian Schulz, "Only My Opinion" by Monica Shannon, and "The Butterfly" by Clinton Scollard, ***Read-Aloud Rhymes of the Very Young.*** (Alfred A. Knopf, 1986).

"White Butterflies" by Algernon Charles Swinburne, and "Hurt No Living Thing" by Christina Rosetti, ***Piping Down the Valleys Wild*** edited by Nancy Larrick (Dell Publishing, 1968).

"Hurt No Living Thing: and "The Caterpillar" both by Christina Rosetti, ***Random House Book of Poetry for Children*** edited by Jack Prelutsky. Random House, 1983.

Poetry Pages *(cont.)*

Innovations

After the children are familiar with a particular poem (see Anthology suggestions, page 49), create some innovations. Underline some words in the original poem and replace them with different butterfly or caterpillar related words. The following Mother Goose rhyme, for example, can easily be innovated.

There was a bee
Sat on a wall
"Buzz!" said he
And that was all.

Rewritten, the poem might look like this:

There was a butterfly
Laid some eggs
"I'm done!" said she
And stood on her legs.

Caterpillar Song

Sing or read the words to the song *"I Know an Old Lady Who Swallowed a Fly."* Discuss some caterpillar words and actions. Divide the class into pairs or small groups and let them rewrite the first two lines of lyrics. For example, "I know an old lady who swallowed a caterpillar; it wiggled and wiggled but still didn't hurt her."

Ideas

With the class brainstorm some ideas about caterpillars and butterflies and record them on chart paper. Here are some ideas you and your class may want to begin with:

- Write words or phrases that tell how a caterpillar moves along a branch.

- Generate a list of words that rhyme with wings, legs, or other butterfly body parts.

- Create a butterfly or caterpillar "menu" of favorite foods to eat.

Have the children incorporate these words and phrases into poems they write about caterpillars and butterflies.

Caterpillar Poem

Cut out some green construction paper circles. Have the children write one sentence or phrase on each circle, using as many circles as necessary to create a poem. Add one more circle for the caterpillar's head. Tell the children to draw facial features on the caterpillar's head. Tape the circles together into a caterpillar shape and put all of the created caterpillar poems on display.

50

Compound Creepy Crawlies

A compound word is made when two words are put together to form one new word. Butterfly is a compound word.

butter + fly

Cut and paste the wings to make some creepy crawly compound words.

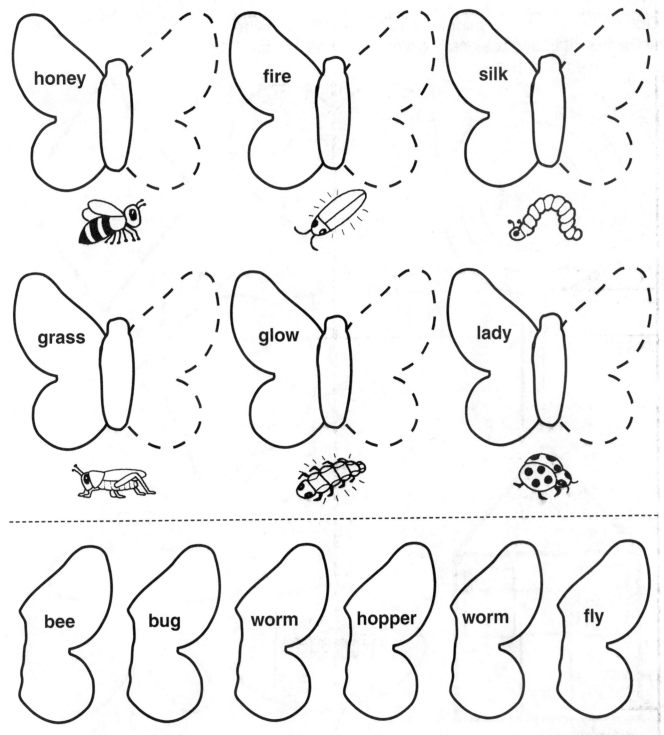

Symmetry

Look closely at the butterfly. Draw a line down its center. Notice how one side looks exactly like the other. This is called *symmetry*. A butterfly is not the only thing that is symmetrical. A drum is symmetrical. A football is symmetrical. Your body is symmetrical, too.

Draw a line down the middle of each picture below to show how it is symmetrical. Color each half so that both halves match exactly.

Hands-On Math

A hands-on math lesson engages youngsters in the learning process. Here are three fun activities for you to try with your children.

Story Problems

Materials

Each child will need a shoebox lid (or a paper plate); a handful of bow tie pasta (with a little imagination they can be butterflies); crayons or markers

Directions

1. Direct the children to draw a picture of a grassy field and two flowers inside their shoebox lid (see diagram).

2. Give each child a handful of the bow tie pasta. Present a story problem, for example, "Four butterflies flew to one flower. Two more butterflies flew to the other flower. How many butterflies were there in all?"

3. Walk around the room and observe the children as they make sets to match the steps of each story problem. As a follow-up have the children work in teams of two making up their own story problems and sharing them with each other as they manipulate their "butterflies" to mathematically match their story problems.

Making Sets

Materials

Green card stock (available at copy stores); copy of page 54; scissors; black marking pens; dried white beans; manila envelopes

Directions

1. Run off copies of page 54 onto green card stock. (Make enough copies so that you will have one set for each pair or small group of children.)

2. Cut out each set of cards. Store each set in its own manila envelope along with a handful of beans which will represent caterpillar eggs.

3. Give one envelope to each pair or small group. Tell the children to make corresponding sets with the beans to match the number on each leaf card by placing the correct number of beans on it.

Hands-On Math *(cont.)*

See page 53 for suggested use.

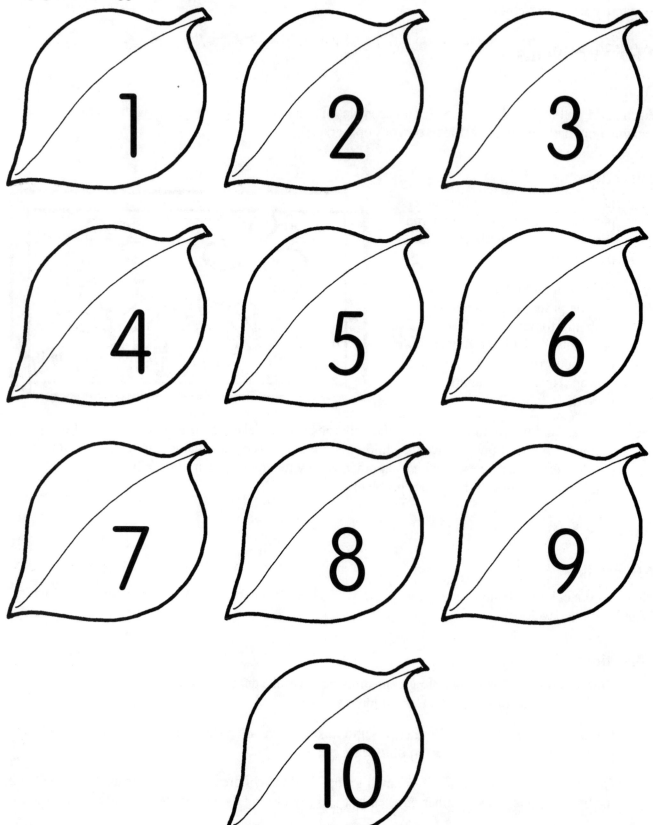

54

Preserving Butterflies

Butterfly collections are truly beautiful to observe. The process of preserving butterflies is painstaking and especially controversial because of the many endangered species. Children can experience a mock butterfly preservation with this fun simulation.

Indoor Nature Walk

Prepare for this activity by constructing butterfly nets (see diagram). Take the children on an indoor nature walk to catch butterflies. Next, place a number of plastic (or paper) butterflies around the classroom. Let the children catch the butterflies with their nets. After the hunting is over, preserve their captured butterflies in gelatin (directions follow).

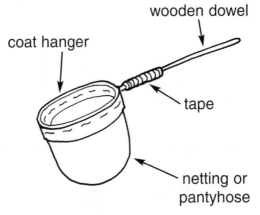

wooden dowel

coat hanger

tape

netting or pantyhose

Preserved Butterflies

Materials

Plastic butterflies (if you cannot find locally, contact The Oriental Trading Company at 1-800-228-0475); lemon or orange-flavored gelatin; water; access to a stove top (or hot plate) and a refrigerator; a wooden spoon; ladle or small measuring cup; small plastic margarine cups and their covers

Note: Because of the potential danger involved in stove tops and boiling water, it is advised that this project be conducted in small groups with close adult supervision.

Directions

1. Make one batch of gelatin according to the directions on the package; use a ladle or small measuring cup to pour a small amount of the liquid (approximately $\frac{1}{2}$" [1.3 cm] thick) into each margarine cup. Chill until the gelatin just begins to set.

2. Place a clean plastic butterfly on top of the gelatin in each cup. **Note:** Make sure the *underside* of the butterfly is facing up. Return to refrigerator and chill the butterflies and gelatin until completely set.

3. Make a new batch of gelatin and add another layer of gelatin over the butterfly layer in each cup; cover and chill again.

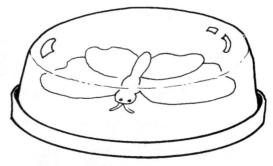

4. Remove the "preserved" (encased in gelatin) butterflies from their containers by dipping the still-covered container briefly halfway into a small bowl of hot water and then turning the container over. Carefully pry apart lid from container. The preserved butterflies should land on the plastic lid display.

5. Remind the children that their preserved butterflies are not edible, but enjoyable to observe!

Butterfly Gardening

An ideal hands-on activity for your butterfly unit is a butterfly garden. There are over 700 North American native butterfly species that you can try to lure to your home or school. It will help if you know what they like. Here are some important facts about butterflies and their preferences, how to plan a butterfly garden, and which flowers to plant. The results will be truly rewarding.

Just the Facts

1. You do not need expensive or exotic varieties of flowers. The list on page 57 outlines some of the more common flowers that will attract butterflies. Find out which of those flowers grow in your area.

2. Butterflies especially like flowers that have clusters of blooms so that they can sip the nectar from as many blooms as possible in one stop. Queen Anne's lace and yarrow, for example, fit this requirement.

3. Butterflies visit the most fragrant flowers first. Lilacs, viburnum, and heliotrope are some especially fragrant varieties.

4. Scientists have found that butterflies like purple flowers best, followed by yellow, blue, pink, and white. Lupines, foxgloves, nasturtiums, and pansies are quite colorful.

5. Butterflies prefer an informal look with plants of different heights rather than a well-manicured look.

6. Leave the weeds alone—they're often a butterfly's favorite plant! For best results, a butterfly garden should be kept strictly organic. Pick off beetles and other pests that have found their way into the garden, but do not resort to using chemical pest controls.

Pre-planning

1. Do a bit of research to help you choose those plants which will survive and flourish where you live. Know which flowers will best attract butterflies. Find out what time of year is best for planting, what types of butterflies you will be able to find and identify at different times in your locale, and whether or not you need to check your soil types. A local nursery may be able to help you determine your choices and answer any planting questions you may have.

2. Ask friends and local nurseries for donations or slips from their own gardens.

3. Gardens with large purple, yellow, blue, pink and white flat flowers work best to enable butterflies to perch comfortably while dining and sipping their nectar.

Butterfly Gardening *(cont.)*

Procedure

1. Stake out a plot of land on school property. Sketch out a simple map for your garden. If a plot of school property cannot be allocated for a butterfly garden, you can plant a garden in a large child's wagon. Line the inside of the wagon with plastic and fill three-fourths full with potting soil. You may also want to try planting a window box or hanging pots in an outdoor hallway.

2. Plan a series of days in which the class may go outside and work on the butterfly garden. Have the children carefully follow your directions as to what is to be performed, where, and when. You may find it appropriate to reinforce or introduce new concepts about butterflies and their habitat as you build your butterfly garden.

Butterfly Food

To attract butterflies, serve them a meal they can't resist! Make sugar water by mixing four parts of hot water with one part white sugar. Line a pie plate with cotton balls. After the sugar water has cooled down, pour the solution over the cotton balls. Coat the outer rim of the pie plate with cooking oil to stop ants from getting into the sugar water. Set the dish outside by some flowering plants. (For another sugary recipe, see page 11 of the June 1997 issue of *Spider* magazine.)

Ideal Flowering Plants

ageratum	cowslip	marigolds	salvias sedum
alyssum	comfrey	milkweed	snapdragons
alfalfa	daisies	morning glory	sunflowers
aster	day lilies	native goldenrod	sweet alyssum
baptista	dianthus	nicotianas	sweet scabious
blanket flowers	hibiscus	parsley	sweet Williams
buttercups	heliotrope	phlox	yarrow
busy butterfly weed	lantanas	primrose	verbenas
clematis	lilacs	purple coneflower	viburnum
clover	lobelias	Queen Anne's lace	zinnias
cosmos	lupines	ragwort	

Did You Know?

Read and learn some interesting facts about butterflies. Unscramble the scrambled words. Write the word on the lines.

1. When a butterfly rests, its (insgw) _____

   are folded up over its head.

2. The (doby) _____ of an adult butterfly

   has three parts—the (ehad)_____,

   thorax, and abdomen.

3. A butterfly keeps its (gontue) _____

   curled up when it is not feeding.

4. Butterflies taste with their (eetf) _____ .

5. The colors and patterns on a butterfly's wings

   are made up of thousands of tiny (slecas)

   _____ .

6. (moSe) _____ butterflies are able to

   disguise themselves with their (locors)

   _____ .

Camouflage

Because butterflies have many enemies they need some way to protect themselves. Their myriad colors and intricate patterns provide a camouflage to the birds, insects, and spiders who might prey on them. Here are examples of the different types of camouflage that butterflies use.

1. Some butterflies sport false eye spots on their wings. These not-so-real eyes scare predators away.

2. Butterflies that are colored yellow and black, or red and black have an unpleasant taste. Other animals and insects know that they should stay away from these color combinations.

3. A number of butterflies blend in with their surroundings as they take on the shape of a leaf or the color of the leaves and flowers in their environment. This makes it difficult for other animals to detect the butterflies.

To help students better grasp the concept of camouflage you may want to engage them in the two activities that follow.

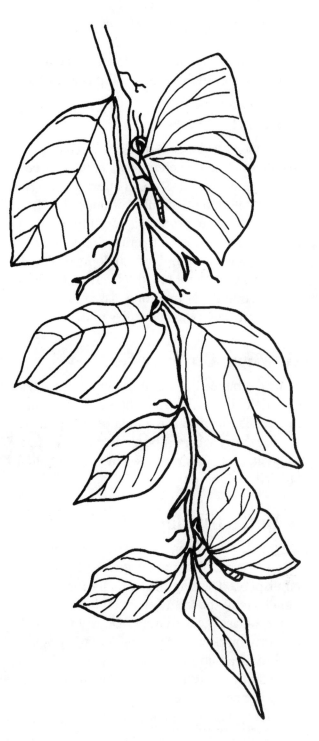

Match-Up

Children can discover how butterflies blend into their background and work on visual discrimination skills at the same time. Prepare ten large index cards by gluing multicolored fabric, shelf paper, or wallpaper samples to each card. Use the butterfly pattern on page 26 to make six butterflies. Cover each one with a pattern or fabric to match the cards. (For more durability you may want to laminate all 12 pieces and store them in a labeled manila envelope.) Introduce the game with the class during circle time. Then place the match-up set at your butterfly center and let the children work independently or in pairs to match each butterfly with its corresponding background.

Pictures

Display some pictures which demonstrate butterflies that are camouflaged. (You may want to use some of the nonfiction book selections listed on page 79.) Discuss how they blend in with their environment. For example, an Indian Leaf butterfly looks like a dried leaf.

Migration

Some butterflies do not live in the same place their whole lives. Instead, they migrate or move to a warmer location. The Monarch butterfly is one such butterfly species that demonstrates this interesting phenomenon. Introduce the children to the concept of migration by reading the book *Monarch Butterfly* by Gail Gibbons (Holiday House, 1989). Follow up with any of these activities and projects.

On the Map

Monarch butterflies are well-known migrating butterflies. In early autumn Monarchs begin their flight south from Canada to places as far away as California, Florida, and even Mexico. Locate these states and countries on a map or globe. Place a butterfly (preferably with the Monarch butterfly's markings) on the map or globe with small pieces of transparent tape.

Butterfly Trees

Thousands of Monarch butterflies can cluster together in one tree creating a "butterfly tree." Create your own classroom butterfly tree. Have each child cut out a number of butterflies from construction paper (you may want to use the pattern found on page 26). Get permission to attach the butterflies to a tree or bush outdoors (be sure to remove them after a few days). If preferred, make a construction paper tree for a classroom bulletin board and attach the butterflies to it.

How Far Do They Go?

Monarch butterflies can travel great distances when they migrate. In order to find out just how far, entomologists (scientists who study bugs) tag and number some butterflies. A butterfly that started out in Canada, for instance, might be found in southern California. The butterfly's tag will let scientists know exactly where it began its journey. Let children speculate where the butterflies in their area have originated. If feasible, ask a local entomologist to come to your class to share more facts on Monarch butterfly migration.

A Butterfly Flag

On the day that Monarch butterflies arrive in Santa Cruz, California, a butterfly flag is put on display. The flag flies proudly for six months until the last Monarch migrates north. Make a class butterfly flag. Draw a freehand butterfly on poster board; cut it out. Have the children wad up small tissue paper squares. Glue the wadded tissue to the butterfly's body using the color patterning of the Monarch butterfly. Attach the butterfly to a coat hanger and display.

Butterfly Eggs

The children may know that butterflies start out as eggs on a leaf. But do they know that butterfly eggs come in a variety of sizes, colors, and shapes? Learn about butterfly eggs. This page contains some introductory lessons and hands-on experiences.

Background Information

Butterfly eggs look different from any other type of egg. They can be green, red, blue, yellow, or brown. Some eggs are round like balls, while others are shaped like little barrels, pancakes, or pickles. Usually their shells are decorated with lines and dots that cannot be seen except through a magnifying lens. The butterfly mother uses a natural glue to attach her eggs to a leaf or fasten them to a twig so they will not fall to the ground. Many butterflies lay one egg at a time, while still others deposit hundreds of them side by side in neat rows.

Experiences

1. Find a leaf. Glue a small white bean to the leaf. Show it to the children and explain that all butterflies start out as eggs on a leaf. Tell the class that a butterfly mother always puts her eggs on a leaf that is her favorite food so that when her eggs hatch there will be plenty of food for her babies to eat.

2. Tell the children that butterfly eggs are very hard to see because they are so small. Explain that butterfly eggs come in many different shapes and sizes. Show the children several pictures of butterfly eggs (see page 62). Explain to them that some eggs are round, some are shaped like cones, some look like gumdrops, and some look like pickles.

3. Let the children make some butterfly eggs. You will need modeling clay or homemade dough in green, blue, red, and yellow. Direct the children to make a gumdrop shape with the green dough. Tell them that this is a Painted Lady butterfly egg. Continue in the same manner with the remaining colored clay:

   - blue pickle shape for egg of the *Common Blue butterfly*

   - red cone shape for the egg of the *Monarch butterfly*

   - yellow tire shape for the egg of the *Spring Azure butterfly*

Butterfly Eggs *(cont.)*

See page 61 for suggested use.

Painted Lady Butterfly

Common Blue Butterfly

Monarch Butterfly

Spring Azure Butterfly

Caterpillar and Butterfly Magnifiers

While it is fun to observe caterpillars and butterflies in nature, it is even more exciting to see them magnified. If magnifying lenses are not available, let the children make their own magnifying tools to better see these magnificent creatures.

Note: Because knives are used in making these magnifiers, you may want to prepare the boxes yourself or enlist some extra help on the day that your class is going to construct these projects.

Materials

An oatmeal container or other cylindrical cardboard container; knife; (optional: tempera paints and paintbrush or construction paper and glue); clear plastic wrap; rubber band or tape; water

Directions

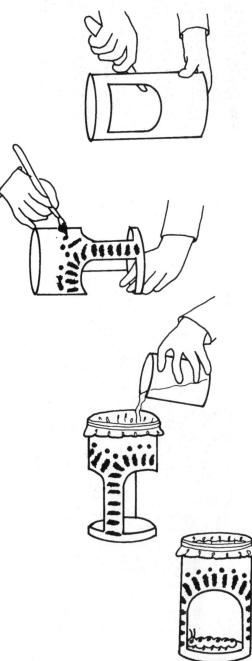

1. Cut away the bottom of the oatmeal container. Discard the lid (if applicable).

2. Cut an arched hole from the side of the oatmeal container. Make the hole near the base of the carton. Be sure that it is big enough for a child's hand to fit through (see diagram). Cut another arched hole from the opposite side of the container. Optional: Paint the outside of the box with tempera paints or cover with construction paper.

3. Tear off a sheet of plastic wrap large enough to cover the top of the carton. Make a slight indentation in the center of the plastic wrap. Hold the plastic wrap in place with a rubber band stretched around the rim of the container.

4. Pour some water into the indentation. In a well-lit area put the caterpillar, butterfly, or other object to be observed on a flat surface. Place magnifier over the object to be observed. Look straight down through the water to view the object.

5. Direct the children to draw a picture of their magnified objects.

A World of Butterflies

Butterflies can be found in just about every part of the world, even in the Arctic tundra and the desert lands of Africa and Asia. Read some interesting facts about these amazing butterflies, then color them. See if you can find where they live on a world map or a globe.

The **Blue Morpho's** metallic-blue wings are sometimes used to make jewelry. It is found only in the tropical jungles of **South America**.

Bright orange wings help the **Orange Albatross** blend into the colorful flowers in the rain forests of **South America**.

The brown **Kallima butterfly** from **India** can imitate a dry leaf.

Colored brown, yellow, and red, **Postman** butterflies of **Central** and **South America** feed first on yellow flowers. Then they move on to red flowers.

Mexico is home to nature reserves where orange and black **Monarch** butterflies spend the winter.

Music-Making

Make music an integral part of your curriculum. On this page you will find some music-making ideas and a list of music resources.

Music-Making Ideas

Discuss with the children the sounds that caterpillars make: when they eat, when they crawl along a tree limb, when they are emerging from their chrysalises. Ask the children to name some sounds a butterfly might make as it wings its way through the sky from flower to flower.

Let the children make some musical instruments that will imitate these sounds. Here are some ideas for you to try:

1. Crumple up newspapers to sound like caterpillars as they move through dried-up leaves.

2. Rub pieces of sandpaper together to imitate the sound of caterpillars crawling along a twig.

3. Slowly rip a sheet of newspaper or butcher paper to make the sound of a butterfly emerging from its chrysalis.

4. Wave a sheet or blanket to sound like a butterfly's wings as it flies. Have the children stand and hold the edge of the blanket as they gently make ripples.

5. Pour some water (no more than one-fourth full) into a paper cup. Give the child a straw and instruct him or her to slurp the water like a butterfly drinking nectar.

6. Put all these sounds together to make a butterfly orchestra. Let the children play their musical instruments as accompaniment to some caterpillar and butterfly songs you listen to (a list of possible resources appears below).

Music Resources

Listen to some caterpillar and butterfly songs and music. Learn the words and music. Choose from the selections listed below:

A Creepy Crawly Song Book by Carle Davis. Farrar, Straus and Giroux, 1993. Includes musical scores.

Animal Piggyback Songs. Warren Publishing House, 1990. Includes "Caterpillar Song" and "Flutter, Flutter, Butterfly."

I'd Like to Be an Entomologist. Twin Sisters Productions. 1-800-248-TWIN or visit them at their website: www.twinsisters.com. A book and cassette set features 12 informative songs that teach children about insects. For ages four to nine.

More Piggyback Songs. Warren Publishing House, 1984.

Beautiful Butterflies

Children can make beautiful butterflies with any of these activities. Choose those which best suit the needs of your class.

Scales and Wings

Tell the children that a butterfly's wings are covered with tiny scales which make up the colors they see. Give each child a butterfly pattern (see page 26). Direct the children to make scales by covering the wings with colored small self-sticking dots (look for them in office supply stores). If necessary, art tissue paper squares also work well.

Spoon and Napkin Butterflies

Each child will need a plastic spoon, a colored napkin (preferably a bright color), and a chenille stick. Direct the children to open up the napkin and gather it in fan-folding style in the center. Place the spoon at the middle gathering point and wrap a chenille stick around the area where the napkin and spoon meet. (This may prove too difficult for small hands so be prepared to have extra help available when doing this project.) "Fan" the paper to form the butterfly's two wings. Use a black marker to draw small eyes on the spoon "head."

Fragile Butterflies

Draw a simple outline of a butterfly on white paper (or use pattern on page 26). Be sure to use heavy, dark lines in the outline. Cover the drawing with a sheet of waxed paper. Have the children trace the outline with colored liquid glue (available in many department stores but if not, make your own by mixing powdered tempera paint with white glue). Allow to dry overnight or longer, if necessary. Gently peel away the waxed paper from the dried glue. Punch a small hole near top of the butterfly and tie a length of invisible thread or fishing line through the hole. For a brightly-colored display hang the butterflies in front of a window.

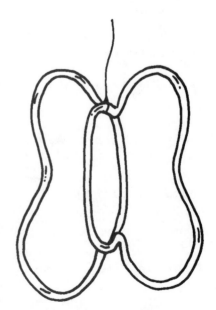

Making Caterpillars

Butterfly art projects are always exciting for the children to do, but caterpillar art projects can be just as fun. Here are two ideas for you.

Foam Caterpillar

Materials

Clean, plastic foam meat trays; small beads; scissors; paper punch; craft yarn; liquid white glue; thin-line marking pens.

Note: If you do not have enough foam meat trays, substitute with colored construction paper or poster board.

Directions

1. Prepare the yarn for threading ahead of time. Cut lengths of yarn and tie a knot in one end, leaving a bit of yarn behind for a tail. Twist the other end into a point and dip it into white glue. Allow the glue plenty of time to dry.

2. Have the children cut circles from the foam meat trays. (You may want to prepare these ahead of time for younger children.) Punch a hole in the center of each circle.

3. Give each child a length of yarn and instruct him or her to push the unknotted end through the hole in a circle. Pull the yarn through until the knotted end prevents the yarn from going completely through the hole. String a bead onto the thread and push the bead until it is touching the foam circle.

4. Continue to thread the yarn in a circle, bead, circle pattern (see example above) until most of the yarn has been used. Knot the second end of the yarn when all the circles have been threaded onto the yarn.

5. Draw a face on the front circle.

Caterpillar Clips

Materials

Small green and red pom pons; glue; spring-type wooden clothespins; black felt or construction paper; chenille sticks.

Directions

1. Glue one red (the head) and three to four green (the body) pom pons to each clothespin (see example).

2. Add felt or construction paper eyes; cut chenille sticks to make antennae; attach.

Butterfly Treats

While it may not be possible—or wise—to eat leaves and drink nectar like butterflies do, children will enjoy making and eating these tasty treats. Sip on commercially-made fruit nectar to complement the food being served.

Bagel Butterflies

Ingredients

Small bagels (one for each child); cherry tomatoes or gum drops; cream cheese; licorice; cinnamon candies

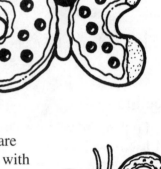

Utensils

Plastic knives; cutting knife (to slice bagels)

Directions

Cut the bagels in half so when the two halves are turned outward two Cs are formed. Place the rounded edges touching one another and connect them with cream cheese. Attach a tomato or gun drop head to the "body" with cream cheese. Cut two licorice antennae and attach them to the head with cream cheese. Spread a little cream cheese on the bagel wings. Place cinnamon candies on the spread cream cheese. Admire the butterflies and then edibly enjoy!

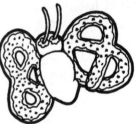

Sweet and Salty Butterflies

Ingredients and Utensils

Small pretzels; candied orange slices; canned frosting; sprinkles; licorice; gum drops or jelly beans; plastic knives

Directions

Cut two slits in both sides of a candied orange slice. (Hint: It is easier to slice when the knife has first been held in hot water for a few moments before cutting.) Press one pretzel into each slit to make wings. Use a gum drop or jelly bean for a head and attach it to the body with frosting. Spread frosting on the wings and body and add some sprinkles. Cut two licorice antennae and attach them to the head with frosting. Yummy!

Butterfly Juice

Butterflies like to drink nectar from flowers. Children may enjoy imitating butterflies by sampling different kinds of fruit nectars from pear to apricot (buy a variety of flavors).

To simulate drinking from a flower, cut out simple construction flower shapes (see sample pattern at right). Poke a hole through the center of the flower and slip it over a straw. Let the children use their flower straws to drink up their nectar juice!

68

Like a Butterfly

Be a butterfly. Give children the chance to experience what it might be like to change and develop as a butterfly. In the process, they will be practicing some important physical skills.

Materials

Crepe paper streamers; scarves (one for each child); pipe cleaners; plastic headbands; party noisemakers that curl up (one for each child)

Preparations

1. Cut lengths of crepe paper long enough to wrap loosely around a child's upper body three or four times.

2. Make antennae by wrapping the ends of pipe cleaners around plastic headbands.

Directions

1. Explain to the children that they are going to experience the life cycle of the butterfly. Tell the children to curl up into a ball and pretend that they are an egg.

2. Tell them that they are growing inside the egg. Then one day a caterpillar begins to emerge from the egg. Direct the children to chomp their way out of the egg, uncurl slowly, and begin to crawl along the floor.

3. Explain that caterpillars need food to grow and so they begin to eat and eat. Have the children pretend to chew food.

4. Now it is time for the caterpillars to build a chrysalis so that they can change once again. Give each child a few lengths of crepe paper streamers to wrap loosely around their arms (children may help one another do this).

5. Tell the children that after some time, a butterfly begins to form inside.

6. Now the butterfly makes its way out of its home. Have the children push out their arms from the crepe paper streamers.

7. Give each child a scarf and a set of antennae to wear. Tell them to gently move their wings as they dry. Then they can flap their wings as they fly away (flapping the scarf as they move).

8. Give each child a noisemaker. Have the children practice slowly blowing the noisemaker out and then slowly letting it deflate. Tell the children that the butterfly has a proboscis or mouth tube that is curled up when it is not feeding. Allow them to use their proboscis to "drink" nectar.

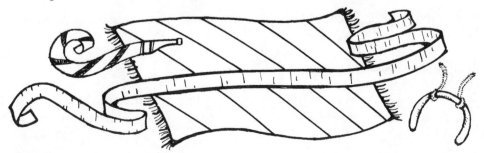

Caterpillar and Butterfly Games

Play some caterpillar and butterfly games to improve coordination, develop small and gross motor skills, and to have some fun! Here are two easy games.

Caterpillar Relay

Materials

Safety cones set up in two identical obstacle courses (This game may be played indoors in a gym or outside.)

Directions

1. Divide the class into two teams.

2. Direct the children to stand one behind the other in their respective teams.

3. Have the children put their hands on the shoulders of the person in front to them.

4. Determine a beginning signal that you will use—a whistle, flag, etc.

5. At the starting signal, children move as quickly as they can (continuing to hold on caterpillar-style), zig-zagging around the cones set up on the racing path.

6. To complete the race, the teams must travel around the cone at the opposite end of the starting point and move back to the starting line. The first team back wins.

Slurp!

Materials

Drinking straws; construction paper; scissors

Directions

1. Use the pattern on page 68 to cut out one construction paper flower for each child (do not cut hole in center).

2. Give each child a straw and a flower.

3. Direct the children to suck on one end of the straw while simultaneously picking up the flower with the other end. Let them see how far they can walk as they continue to suck on the straw while keeping the flower on the end of it.

A Butterfly ABC Book

One way in which to culminate your butterfly unit studies is with an ABC butterfly book. In the process of making the book the children will review everything they have learned about caterpillars, butterflies, and their life cycle. Show the children *The Butterfly Alphabet* by Kjeli B. Sandvel (Scholastic, Inc. 1996) for inspiration!

Materials

Construction paper; colored pencils, marking pens, or crayons

Directions

1. Set aside time for review. During review session(s), ask the children to name words that relate to caterpillars and butterflies. If they need help in remembering topic-related ideas and words, remind them about literature you may have read, videos you have shown, computer programs you have used, or field trips you have taken. Record all responses on the board or chart paper. (It may be helpful to write the words in alphabet clusters for later use.)

2. Prepare sheets of construction paper with a letter of the alphabet written on each sheet; give one sheet to each child. Direct the children to write a caterpillar or butterfly-related word that begins with that letter. (They can refer to the classroom charts that were brainstormed earlier. Also see the Butterfly Alphabet List on page 72.)

3. Have the children draw a picture to illustrate their word or phrase. Encourage the children to use a variety of methods to illustrate their words or phrases. See page 73 for some art ideas. *Optional:* Have the children write their own sentences or dictate a sentence that uses their word or phrase to go along with their illustrations.

4. Create a class book cover with a sheet of construction paper. Place completed letter pages in alphabetical order; bind book with book cover on top. Read to class, then place in class library.

Optional Display

Instead of stacking the pages into a book, make a giant seven [letter] by four [letter] grid (it will look like a patchwork quilt) using all of the completed pages (see example at right). Let all of the children sign their names in the last space (a blank sheet of construction paper); display.

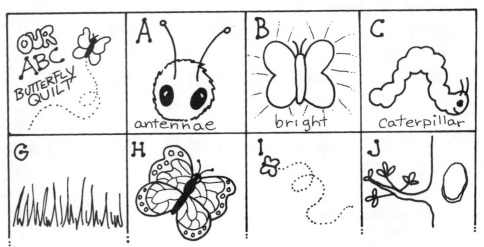

Butterfly Alphabet

Use any of the words and phrases from the Butterfly Alphabet in your Butterfly ABC Book. You may add words of your own to this list.

A	**a**bdomen	**a**ir holes	**a**ntennae	**a**ttractive	
B	**b**reathes	**b**right	**b**ody parts	**b**rittle	
C	**c**amouflage	**c**limb	**c**aterpillar	**c**hrysalis	**c**rawls
D	**d**efenses	**d**ry their wings	**d**rinks	**d**ances	
E	**e**at	**e**ggs	**e**nemies	**e**yes	**e**yespots
F	**f**eelers	**f**light	**f**lowers	**f**ly	**f**ood **f**lutter
G	**g**arden	**g**row	**g**rove	**g**raceful	**g**entle
H	**h**abitat	**h**atch	**h**ead	**h**ibernation	**h**ost plant
I	**i**nsect	**i**nside a chrysalis	**i**magine	**i**sty-bitsy	
J	**j**aws	**J**apanese Swallowtail	**j**ungle		
K	**K**allima butterfly	**k**aleidoscope			
L	**l**eaf	**l**egs	**l**epidoptera	**l**ife cycle	**l**arva
M	**m**ating	**m**etamorphosis	**m**igrate	**m**imicry	**m**outh
N	**n**ectar	**n**ew form	**n**ibble	**n**estle	
O	**o**bserve	**o**rgans	**o**range horns	**o**pen	
P	**p**atterns	**p**oisonous	**p**ollinate	**p**roboscis	**p**upa
Q	**Q**ueen Anne's lace	**q**uickly	**q**uiet	**q**uench	
R	**r**est	**r**adiant	**r**ed	**r**ainbow	**r**hythmic
S	**s**cales	**s**cent	**s**egments	**s**hape	**s**ilken **s**kin
T	**t**aster	**t**horax	**t**ongue	**t**ouch	
U	**u**nderneath	**u**nfolded wings	**u**nbelievable		
V	**v**ariation	**v**ibrant	**v**ery fragile		
W	**w**arm days of spring	**w**atch a caterpillar	**w**ings		
X	**X**erces butterfly	e**x**quisite			
Y	**y**ellow spots	**y**arrow			
Z	**Z**innias				

72

Art Ideas

Encourage the children to use a variety of methods to create pictures for the class butterfly ABC book. In addition to the standard art supplies (tempera paints, construction paper, etc.) you will need a number of other materials. Read through the list of materials below and collect as many as possible for the children to use in making illustrations that are truly unique. Send a note home (use the butterfly pattern on page 26 for stationery) asking for donations of these supplies. Others can be obtained from hardware stores or departments stores, often for free. A sampling of art ideas can be found below the list of materials.

Materials

Lace or other trim, crepe paper, felt, paper bags, wallpaper samples, fabric scraps, colored plastic wrap, craft sticks, cotton puffs, sandpaper, toothpicks, popped popcorn, dried beans and rice, bow tie pasta, shell pasta, cotton swabs, yarn, colored string, colored art tissue, paper plates, sequins or glitter, pipe cleaners, newspapers, straws, colored glue, real leaves and twigs, toilet tissue rolls, pom pons, tempera paint.

How to Make . . .

Caterpillars

Cotton puffs, popped popcorn, or pom pons can be used for a caterpillar's body. Cotton swabs can be cut in half for the antennae or use pipe cleaners. Add fabric eyes.

Flowers

Popped popcorn can be used for blossoms; make a green felt stem and leaves to complete the flower. Cut fabric pieces and wallpaper samples into flower shapes. Add beans, rice, or seeds for details.

Butterflies

Paint bow tie pasta with tempera colors to make butterflies. When they are dry, squiggle some glue on them and sprinkle with glitter.

Chrysalis

1. Crumple up a paper bag. Cut out a chrysalis shape. Paint the paper with tempera paint and sprinkle with colored salt (mix salt and dry tempera paint together) while wet. After the shape dries, tip off the excess salt.

2. Dip string or yarn into liquid starch and wrap around an empty toilet tissue roll. Paint with a watery glue mixture to help the string adhere to the roll; allow to dry. Paint chrysalis with tempera paint.

Wow! Bulletin Board

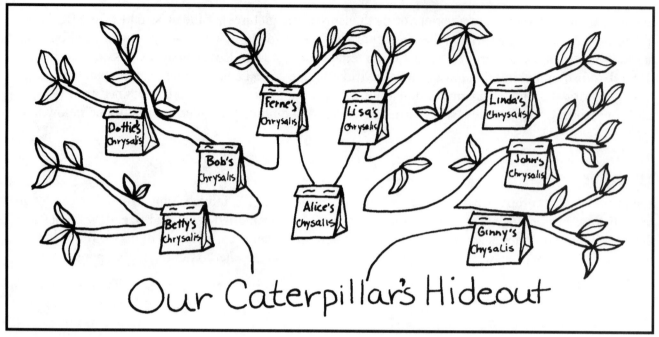

If you want to "wow" your children at the end of their butterfly unit, plan to culminate with this activity:

1. Cover a bulletin board with blue butcher paper. Create a tree with many limbs from brown butcher paper and add green leaves as an accent. Cut out and add the title "Our Caterpillars' Hideout."

2. After you have introduced the life cycle of the butterfly and the specific concept of the chrysalis and its purpose, have each child make a caterpillar (art activity, page 38) that will then be placed into a brown paper lunchbag. On the outside of the lunchbag write the child's name [possessive] and the word chrysalis (example: Janet's Chrysalis). Close and fold the top of the lunchbag down about 1" (2.54 cm). Staple the chrysalis lunch bag onto a tree limb; repeat with all the children's lunchbags. Continue your study of butterflies.

3. About two to three days before your butterfly unit is complete, have the children make small butterflies (possible art activities, page 66). After the children leave for the day (you do not want them to see what you are about to do), complete this task: Study how a child's chrysalis lunchbag is stapled to the tree. (The children have been watching their bags closely and would know if they have been tampered with!) Remove it, open the bag and take out the child's caterpillar. Replace it with the child's just-made butterfly; *this time stapling the top of the lunchbag closed.* Place the lunchbag back onto the bulletin board *exactly* as it appeared prior to the replacing of the caterpillar. Repeat the procedure for the remaining chrysalis lunchbags.

4. On your culminating day, encourage the children to begin to wonder what has happened to their caterpillars hidden deep inside the chrysalises. Remove the lunchbags from the bulletin board and hand them out to their respective owners. (Ask everyone to not open their chrysalis until you give the signal.) When ready, have them open them and watch their faces light up with delight! **Teacher's Note:** Of course the children quickly catch on to the fact that they made those butterflies recently! But the fun and excitement of their discovery is something special to behold.

A Sensational Bulletin Board

Cover your bulletin board area with a butcher paper or burlap fabric background. Make your props (information about patterns and directions below) and attach them to the background.

Materials

A copy of the life cycle story props from page 12 to 14; the directions for enlarging patterns from page 24; overhead projector; transparency sheets; transparency pens; butcher paper; black marking pens; scissors; colored chalk; cotton balls or facial tissues

Directions

1. Follow the directions on page 24 to make the enlarged egg, leaf, caterpillar, chrysalis, and butterfly. Make sure that the outline of each figure is well-defined. Trace onto the bucher paper and cut out each figure.

2. Hold the chalk on its side against the cut butcher-paper figure. Move the chalk around the inside outline of the figure, pressing firmly as you go. Smudge the color with cotton balls or tissue. (To better preserve the pieces, laminate or spray hair spray or art fixative on the colored areas; set aside.

3. Draw a simple tree and branch on butcher paper (see diagram below for ideas). Cut out and color as described in step 2, above. Attach to the bulletin board background.

4. Attach the leaf and the egg to the tree using props during your first lessons or review. The next day remove the leaf and egg; replace with the caterpillar on a branch. On the following day remove the caterpillar and add the chrysalis. Finally, remove the chrysalis and attach the butterfly to the background. On the last day re-attach all of the figures to the bulletin board and add labels for each one (see diagram below).

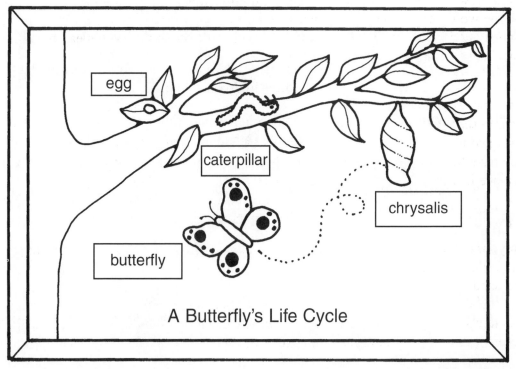

A Butterfly's Life Cycle

Places to Go

Animal zoos have been around for a long time, but a new type of zoo—the butterfly zoo—is just catching on. Introduced to the United States from Europe in the mid-1980s, the idea of a butterfly zoo is becoming more and more popular.

Note: This is not a compete listing of all butterfly zoos. Check in your area for such facilities.

Butterfly Encounter
Museum of Science and Industry. 4801 East Flower Ave., Tampa, FL 33617-2099. 813-987-6300.

The Butterfly Place
120 Tyngsboro Road, Westford, MA 01886. 508-392-0955.

Butterfly World
Tradewinds Park South, 3600 West Sample Road, Coconut Creek, Fl 33073. 305-977-4434.

Cecil B. Day Butterfly Center
Callaway Gardens Resort, Pine Mountain, GA 31822. 800-282-8181.

Cincinnati Zoo
3400 Vine St., Cincinnati, OH, 45220. 513-281-4700. The insectarium houses both butterflies and other insects.

Cockrell Butterfly Center
Houston Museum of Natural Science. One Hermann Circle Drive, Houston, TX 77030. 713-639-4600.

The Discovery Center
231 SW Second Avenue, Fort Lauderdale, FL 33301

Fort Wayne Children's Zoo
3411 Sherman Boulevard, Fort Wayne, IN 46808. 219-482-4610. The Butterfly Jungle is open from late April to mid-October.

Kchuylkill Valley Nature Center
8480 Hagy's Mill Road, Philadelphia, PA 19128.

Marine World Africa/USA
Butterfly Exhibit. Marine World Parkway, Vallejo, CA 94589. 707-644-4000.

San Diego Wild Animal Park
15500 San Pasqual Valley Road, Escondido, CA 92027. Features a hummingbird aviary and 600-700 butterflies.

San Francisco Zoological Gardens
700 Red and Skyline Blvd., San Francisco, CA 94132.

The Smithsonian Institution's National Museum of Natural History
Washington, DC, 20560. Call the Insect Zoo at (202) 357-1386.

Sonora Desert Museum
2021 N. Kinney Road, Tucson, AZ 85743-9719. See butterflies in their natural habitat.

Wings of Wonder, Cypress Gardens
P.O. Box 1, Cypress Gardens, FL, 33384. 813-324-2111.

Resources

On this page you will find a number of science supply houses which sell butterfly supplies. Please contact the individual companies at the number listed.

Carolina Biological Supply

Call 1-800-334-5551 for a catalog.

Dale Seymour Publications

Call 1-800-872-1100 or visit their home page at http://www.aw.com/dsp. Their math and science catalog features a poster of the life cycle of a Swallowtail butterfly, books about nature, and a butterfly garden that is appropriate for all ages. The butterfly garden contains a colorful container for the butterflies, a feeding kit, instructions, and a coupon for butterfly larvae and food (redeemable from the manufacturer).

Delta Education Hands-On Science

Delta Education, P.O. Box 3000, Nashua, NH 03061-3000. Call 1-800-442-5444 for a catalog and more information. In addition to a *Butterfly Garden Classroom Kit,* this company also carries butterfly posters, *Butterflies Abound!* (a whole language resource guide), and a Pre-K-3 activity book which explores protective coloration.

Educational Insights

Call 1-800-933-3277 for a catalog. You can purchase a variety of insect and butterfly-related educational materials.

Insect Lore

P.O. Box 1535, Shafter, CA 93263. Call 1-800-LIVE BUG. Painted Lady butterfly larvae and appropriate nutrients can be purchased from this company. Call well ahead of the time when you will need your larvae as it may take some time to process your order. Check them out on the internet at: www.insectlore.com.

The Nature Company

Dept. CPG, 750 Hearst Ave., Berkeley, CA 94710. 1-800-227-1114. Among the many insect and animal materials it has to offer are raise/release butterfly kits.

Oriental Trading Company

Buy plastic butterflies for prizes, math manipulatives, and art activities. 1-800-228-0475.

Multimedia

It is a difficult task to stay current with all the new technology that is being introduced daily. Here to help you is a list of software, Web sites, and manipulatives that you may want to incorporate into your butterfly unit lesson plans.

Computer Software

Animals and How They Grow. (National Geographic Society, 1993). CD-ROM package. From Macintosh 1-800-567-4321. One whole section is about insects.

Bug Adventure. Floppy disk and MPC CD-ROM. From Knowledge Adventure. 1-800-542-4240. Especially for ages 3-8, this package also includes 3-D glasses, games, and an extensive bug reference section.

Bugs! An Insect Adventure. Available from Educational Resources. Disk, CD-ROM. 1-800-624-2926.

Butterflies Discis. Available from Educational Resources. Disk. 1-800-624-2926.

Butterflies of the World by REMedia. CD-ROM for MAC. Available from Educorp, 7434 Trade Street, San Diego, CA 92121. 1-800-843-9497.

Learn About Insects. For Mac and Apple. From Sunburst. With this program children will identify insects and their parts, dissect and reassemble them, sequence their growth, and match insects with their homes and food. 1-800-321-7511 Monday-Friday 8 A.M.–5 P.M. ET.

The Multimedia Bug Book. For Windows and Macintosh; CD-ROM version is also available. From Expert Software, Inc., 800 Douglas Rd., Executive Tower #750 Coral Gables, Fl, 33134. 1-800-759-2562. This interactive package comes with photos and activities for children ages 6 to 12.

Web Sites

The Butterfly Web Site. http://mgfx.com/butterflies/

Entomology for Beginners. http://www.bos.nl/homes/bijlmakers/ento/begin.html

Gordon's Entomological Home Page. http://info.ex.ac.uk/~gilramel/welcome.html

Videos

Eric Carle: Picture Writer. Available from Scholastic. See how Eric Carle made the caterpillar in ***The Very Hungry Caterpillar.***

Eyewitness. Butterfly & Moth. BBC Worldwide Americans and Dorling Kindersley. VHS video. 35 minutes.